BALTIMORE CATECHISM:

Mass of the Faithful

JOHN T. HOURIHAN JR.

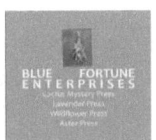

Aster Press
Blue Fortune Enterprises LLC

BALTIMORE CATECHISM: MASS OF THE FAITHFUL

Copyright © 2022 by John Hourihan

All rights reserved. Printed in the United States of America. No part of this book may be used or reproduced in any manner whatsoever without written permission except in the case of brief quotations embodied in critical articles or reviews.

For information contact :
Blue Fortune Enterprises, LLC
Aster Press
P.O. Box 554
Yorktown, VA 23690
http://blue-fortune.com

Book and Cover design by Blue Fortune Enterprises, LLC

ISBN: 978-1-948979-79-5

First Edition: March 2022

Other Titles by John Hourihan

Baltimore Catechism: A Year of Confirmation

Baltimore Catechism: Clean Slate

The Mustard Seed: 2130

The Mustard Seed: 2110

The Mustard Seed: 2095

Beyond the Fence: Converging Memoirs
(with author Amanda Eppley)

Baseball: Play Fair and Win

Parables for a New Age

Praise for Baltimore Catechism: Clean Slate

This autobiographical romp through the Baltimore Catechism is a heartwarming, funny and at times sad memoir of growing up poor and Irish Catholic in the country. Those of us educated by nuns will find some humorous reminders. And in spite of it all, John Hourihan Jr. found his faith. A fun read.

Susan Williamson, author of *Desert Tail, Tangled Tail, Dead on the Trail* and *Dead in the Loft*.

The narrator meets life's difficulties with an equanimity unusual in a six-year-old, and that is the book's charm. No wounded soul here; though he lives with poverty and occasional violence, such elements are but threads in the larger tapestry of his life. That life is nurtured and sustained by his rowdy extended family, especially his mother, and, eventually, the gift of religion.

Karen Cavalli, author of *Bad Mind, Undercover Goddess* and *Down*.

John Hourihan's *Baltimore Catechism: Clean Slate* is a charming account of a precocious child's struggle with his Catholic school first grade year. This fictionalized memoir tells how the boy John struggles with the contradictions in Catholic teachings and the difficulties his family faces. The writing is lively and insightful.

Robert Archibald, author of *Roundabout Revenge, Guilty Until Proven Innocent, Crime Does Not Pay* and *Who Dung It*.

This book is a gem. This story of a young Irish boy trying to understand the seeming difference between religion and reality is laugh out loud funny. But you don't have to be Irish or Catholic to enjoy this nostalgic journey into the past as he struggles to do the right thing.

Patti Gaustad Procopi, author of *Please... Tell Me More*

As a fellow writer of semi-autobiographic fiction, I applaud John Hourihan's new book, *Baltimore Catechism*. Told with the innocence of childhood and the tongue-in cheek irony of adulthood, the book brings out the conflict between religion and reality. Through the eyes of a young Irish-American boy, the book explores what it means to be religious. The author's sardonic whit, coupled with his poignant visual, auditory and olfactory images of people, places and events, makes the book an enticing read. This book is a paean to our common humanity and to what is good in all of us.

Christian Pascale, author of *Memories Are The Stories We Tell Ourselves, Poetry of Wonder,* and *Windows of Heaven.*

This book is dedicated to those I wrote it for, my grandchildren: Chris, Alex, Kevo, Liam, Peter, Althea, Bruno, Rory, River, Vincenzo and Viviana

FOREWORD

I am hesitant to write about my high school experience, even in a book of fiction where some characters are total fiction and present to make a point of truth, and others are composites of many people. This story is fictional but based on truth. For those who believe they have found themselves in this book, or for those who believe they have found someone else they know, or something that happened, please understand, this a fictional representation of what created the truth of my youth. This is how the town I lived in affected me. This story is fictional truth. Enjoy.

At the beginning of the Catholic Mass, the faithful recall their sins and place their trust in God's abiding mercy. The Kyrie Eleison is said, a Greek phrase meaning, "Lord, have mercy." To me, the Mass was divided into two parts, the Mass of the Catechumens and the Mass of the Faithful. Catechumens, those being instructed in the faith, were dismissed after the first half, not having yet professed the faith. This no longer happens, but as a parochial school student I was taught that profession of faith was considered essential for participation in the Eucharistic sacrifice.

Chapter One
THE PROMISE

I FIGURED OUT EARLY in life that it is best to learn the rules before you try to play the game. Parochial grammar school taught me some rules I was supposed to follow. The Sisters of the order of St. Joseph taught the laws of the Baltimore Catechism, augmented by my sainted grandmother Rose Briget O'Flynn Hourihan herself. Now, I was to be tossed into the secular humanism of public high school where I would get to profess my faith in those rules. Or not.

Public high school was about to teach me that knowing the rules and trying to adhere to them only works when they are good rules. I also found out that most rules of law and religion are made by men with very earthly agendas fitting their own prejudices. I learned that no matter what I promised my mother, I was still just "an Irish punk from

Milford" in the eyes of some of the people in the White Anglo Saxon Protestant town of Hopedale, Massachusetts, where outsiders were considered enemies.

By my first year as a teenager, we had moved so many times I began to identify with gypsies. My mother, Sweet Genevieve to most people, although her name was really Mary, agreed her family may have moved from Southern France and through Eastern Europe before moving to Canada, so perhaps we were gypsies.

I had seen the black and white newsreel about the gypsy queen Eliza, dying at ninety years old and having all her possessions burned with her, including her pony. The pony thing stuck with me. I mean, who the hell burns a pony? However, the thing that I remembered most was that her successor was seventy-seven and smoked the same kind of tiny white pipe my great-grandmother was smoking in an old picture my mother had of her. Like the Gypsies, no matter where we landed, it seemed the people who lived there could easily think of a reason why I shouldn't be there.

My family of Irish Catholic Gypsies was moving to the predominantly WASP town of Hopedale.

"Lord, have mercy."

My mother had told me to hold off when I approached her a year or so earlier, on the day of my confirmation, with the suggestion that I transfer from the parochial school of St. Mary's to the public school, Milford High. After nearly a decade of Catholic education, I had felt it was time to move on, get off the instructional merry-go-round, and step out of the spiritual world and into reality. I never expected the two would be so inexorably linked.

Mum said at the time that we were "probably going to move to a different town soon anyway." I took her at her word, since in my thirteen years of life my family had already moved ten times. This, of course, would be the eleventh.

What remained of my family moved to Hopedale right in the middle of my freshman year of high school.

I could still remember the tenement on Canterbury Street in the city of Worcester where, at two or three years old, I had enjoyed scooting down the small hill in the backyard, slithering under the fence, and crawling out to the rail bed of the train tracks of the Grafton & Upton railroad to sit next to the passing train. I liked the wind from the train as it flew by only about ten feet from where I would sit in the grass, just off the gravel. I remember the day the train actually stopped before getting to me. The guy with the funny hat hopped down from the engine. His boots crunched in the gravel bed as he landed, and he proceeded up the hill. He asked, "Do you live in that building?" He pointed to my house. I nodded. He went up and had words with my mother about her toddler sitting so close to his train tracks. She told him, "He likes to feel the wind." He shouted at her until she explained what would most likely happen to him if she told my father, Scrapper Jack, what he had said. He climbed back up into the engine, and the train heaved a sigh of relief as he left.

I remembered clearest the hovel in the woods in Milford where we had moved on my fourth birthday, and how the bank took it away just after my father lost his job at the shoe shop, and our family of nine learned to feel the righteous hunger that comes with your Irish father standing up to the unfair treatment of the influx of Portuguese people to our town. The shops underpaid the Portuguese workers. My father fought for them, helped usher in a union, and lost his job. No matter what, if you were in the right, my old man would fight for you to be treated fairly. In that way, he was a true warrior.

After the bank swiped our house, we lived in a string of apartments where the landlords didn't mind seven kids destroying their property for a while, until they did, and we were asked to leave.

This was followed by a violent year in a barrio in Arizona that tore our family apart, and then a few more apartments in Milford. At the last one, my father's distant cousin let us know our urchin circus was no longer welcomed in his third-floor rental. We had moved to Hopedale, a town my Scottish-French mother lived in as a child and had often spoken of as a paradise. Of course, she remembered it this way because she had been rich and Scottish, not poor and Irish.

By this time, my oldest sister Patty worked at the supermarket to pay her tuition at Worcester State Teachers' College, Diane had married at the age of sixteen, and Sheila and Nancy had been forced to drop out of school for financial reasons and were working in the shoe shop. Nancy also had a second job as a waitress, and I hardly ever saw my sisters any more. I guess I wasn't sure what they

Baltimore Catechism: Mass of the Faithful

were doing with their lives.

Since the move to Arizona to better my father's chances of getting a job and to cure my brother's asthma, and our return to Massachusetts for my family's spiritual and mental health, we were no longer one large entity. We were, sadly, just several people living together. Of the seven children in the family, only myself, Dennis, and Neil would be returning to a new and unexpected school.

My family bought a house on the strength of the paychecks of my parents and my sisters. This house was the first one we had owned since Purchase Street. Mum had told the girls that if they gave their paychecks, or at least a share, for five years, we could own this home. They reluctantly agreed.

The week before we moved there, Mum, Dad, Sheila, and I took a ride through the town. It was beautiful. It had tree-lined streets with plowed sidewalks, an expansive town park, and a lake in the middle where kids were skating. It had three stores, no traffic lights, a single one-way street, and a huge red-brick building in the middle that Mum said was just called "the factory" or "Draper's." My mother pointed out that her father used to work there as a boss in charge of the carpenters, and Dad added, "because he wasn't Irish," and I realized this was where my father had stolen the "Irish Need Not Apply" sign that had for so long hung in our barn on Purchase Street. Dad had once worked at Bickford shoe in the day time and in Draper's foundry at night. When he found payday came in the form of an envelope of cash, he applied for the job under the Italian name of his friend. He got fired because the boss found out his real name when someone recognized him from his days playing basketball for Company I, the National Guard troop in Milford. This made me a little nervous, since, number one, the Italians were welcomed in this town, but the Irish weren't, and number two, my father, being designated 4F for flat feet, was never in the National Guard but was the center on its basketball team.

The church sat right in the center of town. Like St. Mary's, it was a huge stone building. Like St. Mary's, it had stained-glass windows and a huge front door. Like St. Mary's, it was huge and solid and an imposing sight that seemed to demand obedience. As we passed it, I saw a sign that proclaimed in gold letters, "Unitarian." I assumed, unlike St. Mary's, it wasn't a Catholic church, and I wondered if the people here believed in a different god from mine, and that led me to wonder if people could be good without God at all.

The house my parents were buying sat about four miles south of the center. A gray, ranch-style home, it sat beside the concrete company with its ever-present stream of big yellow cement trucks lumbering by our house. It was a mile away from the pig farm and right beside the Hopedale airport where mostly small planes took off and landed, bringing people to visit the factory. The first things I noticed about my new town included the noise, the danger, and the smell of pigs.

The house had eight rooms and two bathrooms on three floors. Everything worked, and I found nothing seemingly similar to the first home we had owned. There was no barn, no dog, no chickens, no garden, no rabbits, no blackberry bushes, and, as I said, everything worked, even the septic system, the furnace, all the plugs, and the player piano downstairs.

This town was about to prove it bore few similarities to anything I had experienced before.

We had moved in January. I never said goodbye to any of my Milford friends. We simply packed up a few days after my father stuffed the Christmas tree out the third-floor window of our apartment in a drunken furor, and we moved everything we owned to Hopedale.

Yippee-i-o-kayay.

On the famous night of the hanging Christmas tree, Dennis and I sat on the couch in the living room and watched. My mother had met Dad at the door when he got home from imbibing a bit o' Christmas cheer at Tibby's Bar, and she said, "We could have used that money for Christmas presents." As much as he liked to drink, she liked to push his buttons. Since we had returned from Phoenix, this was how they communicated. She belittled him, and he fought back. They were just two good people who loved each other but were stuck in a very difficult life.

"You need money for fecking Christmas? Who do you think bought this tree, these lights? Here's your Christmas," Scrapper Jack said as he stuffed the tree out the window and fought with it until it fit outside and swung hanging by the string of lights still plugged into the wall and the metal stand that got hung up on the window sill. We boys laughed a bit. Then Dennis assessed the situation, leaned over to me, and said, "He is in a bunch of fecking trouble."

He stuck his head out the open window.

"Let's go see it from outside," he said, and we bolted.

"Where the hell do you two think you're going?" himself shouted.

"We'll be right back," I said, and we fumbled down the stairs, out into the snow. We trudged through it barefoot and stood in front of the house. Out by the street we drank in our fill of the upside down Christmas tree, fully lit, hanging from our third-story apartment. The multicolored lights reflected off the asbestos shingles.

Dennis, with great ceremony, gave the verdict. "Hanged... by the neck... until dead," he said. Almost on cue, we began to sing, arm-in-arm, "Silent night, holy night, all is calm, all is bright." We continued laughing and singing until I realized we hadn't put on shoes and were standing in the snow, in the darkness.

As I said, only a few days later we moved.

I spent a few days of what was left of Christmas vacation getting acquainted with the son of the man who sold us the house and his cousin, a pretty twelve-year-old girl, who lived next door to me now.

Frannie, the boy, spent hours showing us the intricacies of the woods behind the house and the small airport, whose only runway ran beside our property about a hundred feet from the house. It occurred to me that it was just like my family to live in a place where, if a pilot sneezed when landing, we could all be run over by an airplane.

The girl taught us the tricks of getting into the house if we had the misfortune of losing our key. There were cracks in most of the ceilings, and she explained to us that these occurred because of the deafening noise of the bigger planes taking off. The proximity of the air strip was probably the reason we had enough money to buy the house in the first place.

The girl was friendly. She had short brown hair, bright eyes, and a perfect smile, and I'm sure she had no idea why I had trouble talking to her, but whenever she was around I forgot half the words I knew and kept saying stupid things like, "Is there any place to swim in Hopedale?" That was the first thing I asked her during January in New England. I don't know why I asked her that. I knew immediately that it was stupid, but those were the words that came out. "Hi, hey, is there any place to swim in Hopedale?"

She stared at me blankly for a few seconds, assessing, and then said, "Yes. But not now. It's winter." She spun on her heel and went home. I then spent a few years trying to prove to her that I wasn't an idiot.

Within days, I stood on the stairs in the middle of my house equidistant from both the upstairs and downstairs bathrooms, waiting for a sister to come out of either. It took a while, so I sat down halfway up the flight of stairs thinking, *It's a good thing I don't have to pee.*

Mum walked up and stood on a stair a few steps down from where I sat and said, "Your hair is sticking up in the back." She licked her hand and tried to make it stay down. "Cowlick," she said, and I nodded.

We both knew a new school would be difficult for me. Despite having lived in eleven different places by my first teen year, this was only the third school I'd had to attend for the first time.

"I know it's hard," she said.

"It is," I said. I was frightened for the first time since a crazy Texan adult, trying to scare my father, plummeted down the cutback roads of South Mountain near Phoenix with all us kids in the back of his pickup being tossed from side to side in the metal bed. I still had nightmares about that, as well as about Sister Mary Patrick's threat to put me in a box and ship me off to China, never to see my parents again.

My mother knew this new town because she had been raised here. So it frightened me when she said, "It's going to be different, but don't let them get to you. You've handled worse."

"Okay," I said, and since a bathroom had opened up, and my sister Sheila bounded down the stairs past us, I started to get up to take her place.

"Wait," Mum said.

I stopped and looked down the stairs at her.

"It is a good time to remember the good and get rid of the bad?" It sounded mostly like a question.

"What?"

"They don't know you. You can be anyone you want now."

I didn't answer.

"You know all the rules. You know you can handle anything if you try. Do you know what I mean?"

I did. In Milford, I had learned the Ten Commandments and The Apostles Creed, and in Arizona, I had learned it was necessary to also fight, steal, lie, and cheat every once in a while if I wanted to survive.

"You think I should turn over a new leaf," I said, smiling at her. "Leave out the stuff I learned in Phoenix?"

"Yes," she said. "Maybe turn over a whole new forest." She laughed a bit, but we both knew what she meant. I had learned a lot in the Arizona desert.

Nancy and Sheila kissed Mum goodbye and ran out to the front, where their ride to work waited in the driveway. Dennis and Neil were ready and waiting for Pat and Mum to drive them to the elementary school, and I stepped outside and walked to the bus stop at the end of our road.

The walk was a quarter mile of ankle deep, salted gray slush. As I approached, I saw a handful of kids waiting in the biting cold for the bus. They all individually became aware of the strange kid walking down the hill alone to join their group even without being asked. Then I saw a friendly face. She waved, and the rest of the bus riders turned to her for an explanation. By the time I got there, Cecelia must have told them who I was because they all nodded, or in some way acknowledged my existence. I wanted to thank her. I wanted to let her know how that little wave had made my life easier. I wanted to hug her.

Only one word came to me. "Cold," I said.

She nodded. "Not swimming weather," she said, and she laughed.

I felt as if I had "IDIOT" written all over my face. Then,

thankfully, the bus came.

I was on my way to General Draper High School for the next chapter of my life, uncertain if I would fit in this place like I did in the barrio in South Phoenix, or if I wouldn't fit in the same way I didn't in the rich neighborhood up in north Phoenix. I wondered what it would be like. As the bus bounced down the highway toward my new social life, I couldn't have known how different this experience would be—and how much the same.

Oh right, the thing about my mother's names, Genevieve and Mary. When she was born, she was named Mary, but when the paperwork was to be filled out at her Baptism, her godfather decided he liked the name Genevieve better, since it was the name of his girlfriend, so that's what he wrote on the papers. That is when she became Genevieve.

I guess people back then weren't such sticklers for paperwork, even when the paperwork had to do with God.

Chapter Two
PLUS ÇA CHANGE

AS I STEPPED FROM the school bus at the curb in front of the large brick school with the huge cupola on the top, I surveyed the snow-covered lawn and the crowd of kids between me and the front steps. The shoveled walkway lined with people presented a veritable gauntlet. I intended to stiffen up and walk through them to the entrance stairway, and then to the office for instructions, but my intentions did not happen.

"You Hourihan?" I already had to deal with the questions, even before getting to the crowd, by a tall, thin, blond boy, and wondering how he knew my name.

"Yes," I said.

"I'm Del Palumbo. I'm supposed to show you around today. We have most of the same classes. Come on. We're in Mr. Ty's homeroom." He turned and led the way through the closing crowd of inquiring eyes. At first, I wondered how he knew me, but then I realized I was the only person in the school who every other person in the school did not know. Without knowing how the others felt about that, I figured I would find out soon enough.

As we entered the classroom slated to be our homeroom, located on the first floor of the school, Del, my guide, started introducing me around. He seemed to be well liked by everyone, which worked out well for me because he acted as if I was his long-lost friend and introducing me to his other friends.

Suddenly, the teacher entered and everyone sat down. Mr. Ty called the roll, holding his coffee in one hand and his plan book in the other. With a balding head and a dark blue suit that probably used to fit him, he wore the widest tie I had ever seen around his neck. This tie was wide enough to have a picture of a guy fishing on it, and the scene included half the river. When he got to my name, he glanced up from the book for the first time, squinted through his bifocals, and said, "New?"

"Yes," I said, and the entire class looked at me. It felt like a bad dream. I checked to see if I had remembered my pants.

The "bell" buzzed, and we went to our first class: Mr. Wood, algebra.

As I entered the class, followed by Del, a kid in the front seat grabbed my arm.

"You got a quarter?"

"I do," I answered.

"Put it on the desk. Del will explain."

I reluctantly put a quarter on his desk and headed for an open seat. Only one thought ran through my head. *In Arizona at least they waited until you weren't looking to steal your money.*

As the teacher fumbled through books and papers and put his lunch away in the book closet, Del, who had sat behind me, leaned forward and said, "He likes to ski."

"What? Who?"

"Mr. Wood. He likes to ski, and he does deep knee bends when he talks. We count them, and whoever comes closest to the number at the end of class wins the money."

"So where's my number?" I asked.

Del handed me a small piece of paper with "11" written on it.

The kid hadn't stolen my money after all. This school was going to be okay, I thought, and just as I turned toward the front of the class, Mr. Wood asked, "Do you have a question, Mr. Hourihan?"

"I do," I answered, as I cheerfully turned to fully face the front of the class. "What's algebra?"

Although there were a few laughs, I was met with mostly silence from my new classmates.

The teacher made two fists as if he were holding ski poles and bent his knees as if getting ready for a mogul.

"You didn't take algebra in the first half of the year at Milford High?"

"I didn't go to Milford High." Remembering my promise to my mother, I smiled.

For some reason, the teacher seemed to have decided I was giving him a hard time, when I was only telling the truth. I hastened to add, "I went to St. Mary's. We took Modern Math."

Now it was his turn. "What is Modern Math?"

I searched my mind for an answer, and by some kind of miracle, it came to me. "Set theory," I answered.

"Well then, this is going to be difficult for you. Pay attention. Do your homework."

I couldn't help thinking, if he had done *his* homework, he would have known I went to St. Mary's, not Milford High. *This school,* I thought, *is teaching the old ways, unlike some of the more progressive schools like St. Mary's, but somehow the teacher believes he is the one in the lead.* As he dipped a second time, he seemed to be appreciating the smiles on the faces of the other students in the class. He obviously thought they were laughing *with* him.

Good school, I thought.

"Hand these out," he said to the kid who had taken my quarter.

And there it was. The first thing I saw on the nearly full piece of mimeograph paper:

$5(-3x - 2) - (x - 3) = -4(4x + 5) + 13.$

I thought, *What's the set and what's the subset?*

Mr. Wood walked down the aisle and put out his hand for my paper. "See me after school," he said.

I hadn't done a damn thing, and I was being punished. I sat back in my chair and decided I would count his deep knee bends for the next forty minutes. He did it sixteen times. I had to stay after school so he could tell me to turn to page one and start reading, and I lost my lunch money, all in one period. *Strange place*, I thought.

Next we had history and then Latin before lunch.

I followed Del to the back of the room in history class and sat against the wall. For the new kid, the first, and most important, thing to do is remain anonymous for as long as possible until the rules and the people become clear, but as soon as the teacher entered the room, he stared directly at me. "What are you doing?" he asked loudly, as if I should know what I was doing. I barely knew where I was.

I had no idea what he meant and sat still, as confused as a squirrel trying to cross in front of a car. Indecision made me immobile.

"Who told you to sit there? Get up here!" He pointed to the first chair in the row. I stood, and under the scrutiny of the entire class, I walked to the front and sat back down. My first day turned out to be quickly turning into a nightmare.

He squinted at me for a few seconds and then opened his book. I had seen a power-look before, but my father had a lot more intimidating look. This teacher's look needed work.

I perked up a little when the teacher, a young skinny, skeletal guy with close-cropped blond hair, announced we would be discussing Jim Crow laws.

I knew my friend Buster had been afraid of this guy Jim Crow. I didn't know, however, that this Crow was known all over the country and even featured in history books. I knew Buster because he dropped off and picked up hats when my mother did home work for the hat shop. My parents liked him, and I got to sit on the bumper of his truck with him and split an orange soda. I asked my father once what Buster's last name was, and he had told me, "He only has one name." I asked why, and he had said, "Jim Crow."

"What do we know about Jim Crow?" skeleton guy asked.

Might as well go for it, I thought, remembering my promise to my mother. I raised my hand.

"Yes, Mr. New Person… Hour hand." He said it as if he were talking about the hand on a clock. I felt it wasn't an honest mistake.

"It's pronounced Hourihan," I said. "Like, a whore in the hand is worth two in the bush." I was echoing a family joke told to me by my older cousin. "If you're going to make fun of my name," I said, "at least do a good job of it." He didn't seem sure what he should say next, so I pushed on and answered the question he had asked. "He told negroes they could only have one name, and they did it. So he must have been tough."

The teacher laughed, but not a friendly laugh. It was obvious he wasn't laughing *with* me. "And what makes you think that?" he asked.

"Well, my mother worked at Lish Hat Shop, and the guy who brought the take-home hats to our house was a negro. His name was just Buster, because of this guy, Jim Crow."

"This guy?" he asked, and a broad sardonic smile lit

his face. I saw the rest of the class had the same smile. This time, they were laughing *with* the teacher. It would turn out later that most Hopedale natives practiced and perfected this sarcastic smile.

"Yes, Jim Crow. He must have been a white guy, because he had two names."

"Are you being a wise ass?" he asked me and started slowly toward my desk.

"No," I said. "What did I get wrong?"

He shook his head and turned back to the front of the class and began collecting answers from the others in the class.

It made me more nervous than I had been in a long time. I raised my hand.

"Yes," he said. "What now?"

I had no idea why he seemed to not like me, since he had only met me a few minutes ago.

"Can I go to the boys' room?"

"May I? And no. This is only second period. You should have gone already."

I had been through this before, in the first grade. I didn't understand how any human being could have the power to decide when another human being could do the most natural thing a human being could do. Take a leak. I mean, God created us to function this way, and for human beings to try to force us to stop working the way God made us was just plain torture. I didn't think teachers were allowed to torture their students.

"What?" I asked.

"Hearing problem? I said, no."

"Why not? And why are you being such a... pain?"

He put his book down on his desk and turned to me.

He spoke, enunciating each word precisely. "You cannot go to the boys' room." He took a step closer. "You now have a decision to make. Either you sit quietly, or I send you to the office. Maybe it's a new rule for you, but here you go to the rest rooms between periods."

I thought someone might have told me that before I had to go.

He picked up his book and stared into my silence. After a few seconds, he opened the book and all I could think of was, *I'm sorry, Mum. I guess my new leaf turning will have to begin tomorrow.*

I had long ago decreed that people didn't get to decide when I got to go to the bathroom. If I had to go, I had to go. It was only human.

"No," I said.

"No what?" He spun around as if he had been hoping for me to say something. He stormed to a point between my seat and his desk. "No what?" he asked again.

"No, I don't have a decision to make." I said. "You have a decision to make. Either you give me a pass to the bathroom, or I go right here. There is no decision, just biology. It's how God made us."

I'm pretty sure nobody in the room expected this answer.

"God, huh? Go to the office," skeleton man said.

I stood up, and as I walked down the aisle, I peered directly into his eyes and said, "You don't mind if I take a leak first, do you?" I meant on the way to the office, but he jumped out from in front of the desk just in case.

"Get moving!" he said.

In the hall, I realized as bad as this day had begun, it could get worse. I went to the bathroom, and then I walked out the front door of the school and walked the frigid four miles to my new home. I figured a do-over might be in order. I'd try this again tomorrow. I had a promise to keep.

Chapter Three
A NEW SET OF RULES

THE NEXT DAY, DELL met me again as I stepped off the bus. This time, he did not smile.

"Man, you're in trouble," he said, as we walked toward the building.

"Why?"

"Are you kidding me? You were sent to the office, and you didn't go. And you left school in second period."

"Oh," I said. "So where do I go, the principal's office or homeroom?"

"Homeroom, I guess."

I wasn't in my seat three seconds when Mr. Ty said, "Don't even sit down. Mr. Kent is waiting for you."

I almost said, "I'm already sitting down," but decided against it. Instead, I got up and left for the office. I guess they weren't done. As I walked to the front door of the classroom, I noticed there were no smiles now. The faces in homeroom seemed to be collectively confused, as if no one had ever said "no" to these people.

The huge, deep brown oaken door of the principal's outer office stood open, and there were a few thick wooden chairs inside that had most likely been made out of the same kind of wood as the door. There were two more doors inside the waiting room, and the three chairs were between them. I sat down, and no sooner had my butt hit the seat than a large, gray-haired man stepped out of the door to my left.

"You wanted to see me?" I asked.

"Not me," he said. "I'm Mr. Dooley. I'm the vice-principal. Mr. Kent wants to see you. He's the man in charge." He pointed to the door on my right. "Knock first, and wait for his answer. Good luck."

When I knocked on the door, I realized the intensity of my trouble was probably more than I initially thought.

"Come in, Mr. Hourihan," said the voice behind the door.

The voice boomed, deep and commanding, and I wondered how he knew who was knocking. I pulled the heavy, formidable door open with two hands on the large, round brass doorknob and immediately felt the weight of the room. The stiflingly hot air engulfed me, a nearly visible thing. As I held the door open, the sun glared in from the windows behind the man and momentarily dimmed my vision. The morning light made the air visible, like a mist in the room. My armpits were giving up my attempt to not sweat, and when the door thumped closed behind me they gave up completely.

I shot a glance behind me at the closed door, and when I turned back, there, sitting behind the huge desk in front of the large pair of windows, was the principal, Mr. Kent.

He was a small man, bald and bespectacled and seemed more like a desk ornament than the creature his voice, when it was behind the door, had promised.

Only one phrase ran through my head. *Pay no attention to the man behind the curtain.*

"Sit down," he commanded.

I sat in the tiny chair in front of his desk, and he stood up so he could better stare down on me. He walked around the desk.

"Do you play baseball, Mr. Hourihan?" he asked, and I thought, this might not be about yesterday at all.

"Yes, sir, I do. I played for…"

A wave of his hand showed he had no interest in anything I might say about pitching for the Phoenix All-Stars. So I stopped talking.

"So, you know you get three strikes, right?"

"Yes sir."

"Well, you are an Irish punk. That's one." He turned his back to me and looked out the window. "And you are an Irish punk from Milford." He turned back toward me. "So that's two strikes, right?"

I didn't answer. Clearly, he saw himself as the umpire in this scenario.

"So, you get one more strike, you Irish punk from

Milford, and then you are out of here." He turned quickly toward me and bent down, putting his face right in front of mine. "Get it!?" he almost shouted.

I did get it. He didn't think of himself as the umpire. He thought of himself as God.

I had promised my mother, and it was a rule that when you promise something to your mother, you should try your best to do it. He must have felt my attitude adequately subservient, and so he let me go to my first period, which thankfully did not include history today. Instead, I had Latin.

As my heels clicked on the spit and polished tile floor in the hallway, I began to enjoy the sound, and before I knew it, I was at the doorway to my Latin class. It had already started.

I tried to be as invisible as possible as I walked between the teacher and the class of fifteen or so kids, all following my every move as I hustled to the nearest empty chair, which happened to be the farthest from the door. Just as I settled in my chair, I noticed the teacher, a heavy, balding, middle-aged man, who focused his attention on me. When I must have seemed to be more comfortable than I was, he said, "I have a few questions for you. You are…" He flipped a page in his planner book and said, "You are John Hourihan?"

I nodded.

"Nice Irish name," he said. Then he paused. "First, how come you're late?"

"The principal wanted to… welcome me," I said. I

could hear the nervous twittering behind me from the class.

"Okay. Second question, how do you pronounce this word on the board?"

Large, printed letters on the blackboard spelled the word "Caesar."

I wondered if this was some kind of trick, if I was going to be in trouble for how I answered it, so I stalled.

A girl, sitting somewhere in the middle of the classroom, laughed and said, "That's okay, John. We don't know either." It broke the ice and made the tension in my entire being relax. With her acknowledgement, I realized it wasn't a trick. He actually wanted, for some reason, to know how I pronounced it.

"Seezer," I said.

"Good," he answered. "I was afraid coming from a Catholic school you might still pronounce it Kaizar. The Catholic schools used to pronounce it like that. There would be a whole bunch of pronunciations that… well… never mind. It's just good."

He went to the closet and got me a Latin book, walked it over to my desk, handed it to me with a smile, and went on with his class.

I opened the book and saw, "All Gaul is divided into three parts." The book at St Mary's had the same opening. I knew a few lines down would read about how the Celts fought the Romans. I wondered if the teacher would even talk about Boudica, the Celtic warrior princess who fought off the Romans. The familiarity made me feel more comfortable than I had felt since I had opened the front door of the school for the first time.

When the buzzer announced the end of the class, everyone streamed for the door. When I walked by his desk, Mr. Katz said, "Hey, Hourihan." I stopped and turned to see him smiling again. He held up a finger to pause the conversation until the classroom emptied. When we were alone, he said, "Don't let them get to you. They don't like me either. I'm a Jew. If you need to talk to someone, stop by."

In my short life, I had been thought of as a precociously dangerous train-loving child, as a very weird looking boy, as a demon, as a Yankee, as a pachuco, as white trash, and now my Irish Catholicism, and the fact that I came from the town next to this one, were to be points of contention. The only place I had fit in at all in my entire life was in the woods and in the barrio.

For weeks, I managed to slide into the conglomerate of students in this new school. I made friends with a few kids, and then my test scores, taken days before I started school here, came back.

I was sent from Mr. Ty's homeroom to the guidance office, where a nervous young man told me that I had done well on the tests. The guidance counselor seemed genuinely surprised.

"It's just that if you haven't been, well, taught here, you know, what's on the test, the Iowa test, well, new people don't usually do very well on their first testing. I guess you will stay where you are in the College Course," he said.

"Are those the smart classes?" I asked.

"No," he said. "We don't track students here. A student, by his test scores, is placed in the College Course, the Business Course, or the General Course. Whichever is best for him or her."

"So I did well on the tests, and I'll be in the College Class?"

His attention was drawn again to the unexpected test scores in front of him on the desk. "Right. You won't have to change classes at all. Go ahead. Go to class. Good job."

I walked to the next class wondering what he thought "tracking" students meant if not this.

At home that night, I pulled a kitchen chair into my bedroom. I sat in front of the window and strained my eyes, trying to see into the darkening woods behind my house. I couldn't see any buildings or a junkyard dog like in Phoenix, or the church like on Winter Street. Instead, I saw trees just like when we had lived in the bucolic paradise of Purchase Street, but here, even when I tried to do the right thing, it backfired. I had felt this way before. When I was the tender age of four years old, my family had first gotten Butch the cat. It seemed to me that this new school state of affairs mimicked the Butch the cat situation.

I had begun to recognize that there were times when I found myself in the dark with a problem, and then I found what I felt was a short-term way out of the darkness, only to find out it was the wrong long-run solution.

I had found that it is possible, even normal for me, to do everything right according to my skill set and knowledge and still get a bad result. It isn't wrong. It's just life. What's wrong is when you realize what you are doing isn't working, but you won't change the plan out of pride or stupid.

And this thought, of course, made me think of Butch the cat.

I had been four years old when we had moved to the Purchase Street farm. Well, it had been a farm when we bought it, but we never really worked it past a subsistence garden and a few chickens and rabbits, so I'm not sure what you would call it. We continued to have chickens until one day my father tried to butcher one for dinner, and when he tried to cut off its head with the butcher knife we had already used to cut the linoleum so it would fit on the kitchen floor, which meant the chicken won the fight. It was where we lived. Nothing much else, just home.

One night, my father and I took a ride with my cousin Joan's husband Bill to a real farm where we picked up Butch.

A pure black Tom, Butch had, only days before, grown out of kittenhood into what might pass for a rather scrawny cat. The adults had to catch him first, and I got a chance to be entertained by three fully grown men chasing a cat in and out of the barn. They ran in the door.

The cat came out the window. They ran out the door, and he zipped through Bill's legs and under the car. I enjoyed it mostly because I had begun to identify with the skinny little rat catcher. Finally, they cornered him and caught him.

I got to hold him on my lap on the ride home in the dark back seat of the black '48 sedan.

Bill started the car, turned on the headlights, and my old man turned around and handed me the cat. He said, "Grab him by the scruff of the neck, like this. Don't let him get away, or we'll be out all night chasing him. Hold him tight."

Even though I had fleeting ideas of letting him go just to watch the men try to catch him again, I grabbed him by the neck and held on tightly.

After about a half-hour, we rumbled down the blackened driveway to our house and parked in front.

Only a few steps inside the yellow light of the kitchen, my mother met us and scowled. "Oh, for God's sake Johnny, don't hold him like that. Cradle him." She showed me how to wrap one arm beneath the cat and put one over the top, holding both shoulders with the top hand.

"He ought to get rid of the rats," my father said, convinced.

"He's barely bigger than the rats," my mother contradicted.

It seemed there were always two sets of truth at my house, which had made my incessant search for a singular truth a futile impossibility.

"Johnny, give him a drink of water," Scrapper Jack said. He and my mother poured themselves a coffee and walked into the next room.

He had no name yet, just "him," or "it," or "the cat," and since this was my first pet, I had no idea how a cat drank water.

I knew horses in the cowboy movies drank from a trough, which we didn't have, and birds drank from a bird bath, which we didn't have, and I knew a glass was a good bet for humans, but this cat had no beak, no lips, no obvious way to drink water.

They continued into the living room.

I stood in the dark of the pantry, next to the kitchen sink.

Cats wouldn't drink hot water, I thought. So there was that. I climbed up to the counter, dragging Butch beside me. He seemed to trust me and sat next to my leg, licking up some spilled canned milk.

"Okay," I thought. "This must be how."

I grabbed the cat by the scruff of the neck, turned him over directly under the faucet, face toward the spigot, and turned on the cold water, full force.

Butch let out a screech, and the blood oozed from a long scratch that magically appeared on my forearm. I turned off the water and let go of the cat, who literally flew by my face, bounced off the front of the stove, scurried into the living room, and hid under the couch.

Everyone turned directly to me sitting in the dark, on the counter, cradling my wounded right arm.

"I guess he don't want any water," I said.

Both my parents, who had seen what I was doing too late to say anything, laughed uncontrollably. Dad even spit out a little coffee.

Now, in the present time, I had a similar problem. That cat never trusted me again. I wanted to get along with these Hopedale people, so I had to feed them a drink that would make them accept me so I could prove my efforts to turn over a new leaf to Mum. It seemed to me the trick would be akin to figuring out how to give a cat a drink of water without getting scratched. It would take more thinking than I had done back then. That cat was long dead but still hated me.

During a lunch period, sometime in April, one of the more popular kids in the class approached me. I knew he must have been popular because he smiled all the time. Most of us insecure teenagers smiled only when we felt we were supposed to, in the hopes that the right people would accept us. He didn't seem to care who accepted him, or he knew everyone did. Either way, that would make him popular. He was the same kid who had asked for my quarter on the first day.

"Hey, Hourihan," he said as he came to the table where I sat with two friends. "Can I talk to you?"

"Sure" I said.

"Not here. Come on," he said and walked off, leaving the cafeteria and stepping into the hallway.

"Don't hang around with those two," he said, nodding

toward the two friends I had been sitting with.

"Why not?"

"Well, just don't. One is strange. The other one's a jerk, and besides, they're just weird. They aren't the right people to hang around with. Have you seen what they do on weekends? They fly model planes, for Christ's sake. Find some new friends." He took a breath and then added, "And buy some new clothes."

Uncertain how to feel about this, I weighed my options. The two kids I had been talking with between classes and eating lunch with were fine, but this other kid was very popular, and maybe he knew something. The whole class had been together since the first grade and knew each other pretty well. It also occurred to me that if I continued to be friends with the two, next week he would be telling people not to hang out with the three of us. And I had no idea why I shouldn't wear my brown corduroys and dark green Salvation Army thrift shop boat-neck sweater.

I took the coward's way out. I stayed friends with the two boys, but also found new friends. Of course, my new friends did not include the kid who told me to find new friends. It was the best I could do.

By May, I had new friends who had signed me up on their bowling team. I thought it strange that they felt knocking down ten pins an acceptable thing to do, but flying model planes ranked as not cool. Fortunately, my mother thought being on a bowling team was a good step in the clearing of the forest, so I went. She paid. For me, a win-win situation. Then the first time I showed up at the Ten Pin alleys, I found out why this was ultimately different from plane flying.

There were girls here.

Girls didn't fly planes or do a lot of bowling, but they did show up at the alley when the boys were having their bowling leagues.

The first day of the league, I walked down Route 140, the three miles to the alleys and met with Peter and Mike, my two new friends; the ones who were acceptable to everyone. We rented our bowling shoes, which were in better shape than my own shoes. If they weren't green and red, I might have walked out with them and left my loafers in the rack. Next, I chose a black ball with three holes in it. It seemed I was a natural middle-of-the-road bowler, which means I cracked 120 in the first string. But after that first string, I realized the real purpose of the Ten Pin bowling alley.

Bowling was acceptable to parents. What happened at the bowling alley wasn't, but parents apparently didn't know that. With the bowling alley came the parking lot, where we spent most of our time. With the parking lot came cars, and with the cars came cases of beer or bottles of Boones Farm Apple Wine and Tango. With the cars, and the beer, and the wine, and the girls, came testosterone-fueled drag races, among other things. When the races happened, you either went, or you were left sitting alone in an empty bowling alley.

Mike, a tall fifteen-year-old, brown-haired son of a

Marine, and Peter, who at fourteen was so good looking he had senior girls asking him out, and I, sat at one of the tables that lined the length of the bowling alley. At a hundred and twenty-five pounds, as tall as Mike's shoulders, and with no perceptible biceps, I seemed out of my element with these two, but for some reason they liked me and dragged me everywhere they went.

Suddenly a buzz of excitement began and grew at the tables, and a commotion started to move through the alleys like a wave. It started as a few boys we didn't know pushed through the side doorway and shouted, "Races!" and everyone rushed out the side door like water pouring out of a faucet into the parking lot.

Mike jumped up and consulted with someone he knew at the food counter. He returned and told Peter and me that the races were in Northbridge at the quarter-mile.

Within minutes, I was being ushered into the back seat of someone's '38 Plymouth, and we were off to the quarter mile. The three-string contest had been abandoned, and the real reason we were at the bowling alley had begun. One of the older kids who got to sit in the front seat turned and handed me a Carling's Black Label. It was the first beer I had ever drunk.

We watched the race between a candy apple red Corvette and a drop-top '50 Ford hot rod. An older girl stood in the road between the two combatants in her tight red pants and white sleeveless blouse. She spread her arms like an angel, and when she dropped them to her sides, the tires screamed, and both cars poured blue, burnt-rubber smoke from all four of their back tires. I was so excited I didn't even know who won, and before I knew it, we were back at "the Ten Pin" and sitting at a table smoking Pete's Tareytons.

Mike sat, pontificating about the Corvette's "195 horsepower, 265 cubic-inch engine" and how it was too powerful for the Thunderbird engine in the Ford that had "292 cubic inches but only 193 horsepower," and I realized I needed to pay more attention to automobile lore if I was ever going to fit in.

A silence fell. It didn't occur to me that someone stood behind me until I saw Mike had stopped talking and his attention had been drawn to a point over my head. Peter, who sat beside me, looked over my head too.

A voice came from behind me.

"That's our table," the voice said.

I turned. I knew the kid who stood there. He was the older brother of one of my Milford classmates. I had never met him before, but I knew he had been in the Marines. By his bald head, I assumed he must have been still in the Marines and home on leave.

"So," he said. "Get out of our table!" There were four others standing behind him. It seemed it might be a good idea to leave. There were other empty tables and, well, he was a Marine.

I stood, getting ready to leave, and Mike said, "Sit down."

He turned toward the Marine. "There are other tables."

"I'll kick your ass, you twerp."

Mike was big, but this guy was bigger.

"I don't think so," Mike said, and he stood up.

"You don't think what?" the older boy asked.

"I don't think you can kick my ass," Mike said calmly, not as a threat, but more like he just didn't think it was possible.

I had had fights before, but this one didn't seem fair. It was my high school friend and a Marine on leave, who seemed to be backed up by some of the toughest kids in Milford. I turned to Mike and said, "Are you sure? I know this guy. He's older than you think."

"I know you," the Marine said, turning toward me. "You're my brother's friend, aren't you?"

I thought maybe we were off the hook and said, "How is he? I haven't seen him since I left Milford."

"How the fuck do I know? Shut up!"

Not off the hook, I thought and wisely shut up.

Mike stepped in front of me and glared at the other boy

"I don't care who you are. I'm sitting at this fucking table, and you aren't going to make me move."

"Outside," the Marine said.

Peter and I followed Mike out the side door. As soon as we got there, a circle of older kids formed, and we were pushed to the back. This happened often at the bowling alley. I walked a few steps into the parking lot and stood on the bumper of a car so I could see. The Marine laughed and threw a punch. Mike moved his head and the punch missed. It was the last thing the older boy did until he went down. Mike, it turned out, was not only the son of a Marine who was fleet champion in boxing, but he was also his father's sparring partner. By the time the fight ended, all the older boy's friends were friends with the fifteen-year-old who had just kicked a Marine's ass without once getting hit himself. It did occur to me that making friends with a badass had always been a very good idea.

The older kids invited us to take a ride with them. They drove to a field in the woods in Milford. Older girls were there, and everyone drank. A lot of the people there were from Milford, and when they heard my name, they began asking about my sisters; whether they were still living in Milford, and were they seeing anyone special.

Then a very large boy a few inches taller than Mike walked up, and one of the kids we were with introduced me to the big kid named Vincenzo. I quickly realized this was supposed to be some kind of a privilege. I was told he had a reputation for having fought five kids at once and won. We both grinned at each other for a few seconds, and then we both started laughing. It was supposed to be a privilege for a little kid like me to be introduced to the toughest kid in all of Milford.

"I know Johnny. We go a long way back," Vincenzo said.

Everyone stood mute. It was inconceivable.

"When I first came to Milford, I had no bike. Johnny tore apart two of his sisters' bikes and put them together to make one and gave it to me. We've been friends a long time."

To tell the truth, I wondered if he remembered that. I was overjoyed that he had.

He slapped me on the back. "Good to see you again," he said and left.

I was instantly verified in some circles as an okay person to be friends with.

Mike and Peter now had new respect for their little friend, who knew some of the toughest kids in the big town. I figured I would ride that for a while.

Saturdays became a ritual. I would get money from Mum, walk to the bowling alley, pay someone to buy beer and ride around with Mike's friends, getting drunk. After sobering up, I went home for dinner.

I was a thirteen-year-old freshman in high school, and, because of my lifelong, under-nourished diet, most of my class outgrew me. I had barely reached puberty, and I was turning over a new leaf as best I could. I found my life from then on would be lived with my friends, school was just something to put up with, and parents were just people to be kept in the dark.

Moonie and Harry Babu were names I heard nearly every night that summer between my freshman and sophomore years. It seemed everyone knew why they were important, except me. Each, it turned out, owned a pool hall in Milford, and the kids from Hopedale saw each as being a rite of passage into manhood.

After begging off for several weekends in a row, I realized

I would have to take a deep breath and follow Mike to Milford and try playing pool. I had played pool only once before when my father had taken me to a bar with him for the afternoon. I wasn't very good at it, so I didn't see much of a reason to try it again. It had, however, become apparent that indecision over whether or not to play pool was retarding my social progress. That decision behind me, I now had to decide which local billiards parlor to frequent. There were rules involved with this rite, and if I wanted to move onward, I would have to learn them. I sincerely hoped they didn't conflict with the rules I already knew.

My friends were spouting new vocabulary that included masse, poon, lagging for the break, scratch, eight-ball, nine-ball, and respecting the Irish. I liked to be respected, so I said the words long before I knew what they meant. I had no idea what they were talking about, but I realized I had to make a choice, and I would have to make it all by myself.

Moonie had been a friend of my old man, and he lived in our neighborhood when we lived on Purchase Street, so I figured we'd go to his place.

But Harry Babu (no one called him just Harry—we called him Harry Babu or nothing) had a cheaper rack and kids from Hopedale usually went to his place.

Moonie cost fifty cents, and Harry Babu was two bits. My spending money would be what I could "scrounge," so I aimed for cheap.

I tried Moonie's first.

Mike and I walked down Central Street on a Friday night. Peter had a date with the prettiest girl in Milford. We kind of hated him for it, but he was our friend so it was okay.

We fought the adrenaline that turned our knees to water as we left the brightness of Main Street and inched shaking into the darkness of an older world of broken streetlights, bars, drunk adults, The Central Street Butcher Shop, and Moonie's.

Lured by the distant iridescent blue of the neon sign, we shuffled down into the coolness of the river breeze and the echo of barking dogs.

"Moonie's" it flashed. And "Pool."

I pushed hard on the heavy door, and it opened with a whoosh of stale air, and an incandescent reddened world of gray smoke floated under green, hooded table lights.

The air clicked and plunked, and I heard the tap of a cue on the table. "Six, cross-side," was followed by the boys of the street calling on their mothers when someone missed or worse, scratched. We leaned against the wall and watched. There were four tables on the lower floor and more up a few steps past the "war room" where the horse boards were behind closed doors.

Grown men played on the upper level. Paper money stacked on the sides of the tables.

One poured whiskey from a bottle into his coffee between shots.

Most of Renda's gang was on our floor, a formidable gang of young toughs, mostly Italians, from the Plains of Milford, and Moonie sat at a table at the foot of the double-wide stairs.

"Hey, you playing or watching," Moonie demanded.

"Playing," I said.

"Five table."

I hung my thumbs onto my pockets and searched around trying to find the table without appearing to be a novice, which is difficult for a thirteen-year-old with the collar of his white shirt up in the back like a pre-pubescent 1950's juvenile delinquent trying to be inconspicuous in a man's world.

Then a kid named Garcia, who had been a few years ahead of me when I had been in school in Milford, motioned to me from a table near the corner.

"This is five," he said, as I arrived, followed closely by Mike.

We might as well have been sucking our thumbs. People chuckled as we pushed by one table and again as I checked the house cues stacked at the side.

Garcia racked, broke, got stripes, ran the table, and tapped with his cue on the edge as he waited.

I put up the cue and turned to go.

"Five bucks," he said.

"What?"

"It's the five table, you asshole."

I didn't like what I had been called, but it sure wasn't the time or place to stand up.

Moonie interceded.

"Hey, brutta faccia, c'mere you."

He opened a thick cloth-bound book and said, "What's you name?"

I told him.

"You Jack's kid?" He smiled.

I was. He reached into his pocket and covered my bet, but now I owed him, and I had no doubt my father would find out I had been here. In the end, I never paid him back.

The next afternoon we went to Harry Babu's, smoked Luckies, and played a quarter-a-game nine-ball.

Where Moonie was a moon-faced, robust Southern Italian with ham hands and a lasagna paunch; Harry Babu was a bony, harried, crypt-keeper-like specter with a raspy voice and with hair and skin too white to be human.

He sat glowing in the dark in the corner, chain-smoking camels and drinking from a red-plaid thermos.

We would go to him before the rack, and his chicken-claw hand would reach out for his quarter. He plunked it into a steel box he kept on his lap and then we'd play. He made most of his money giving pool lessons.

Harry's place cost less and was simpler, but I got the feeling that every day would be just like the last one.

Moonie, however, was beyond my understanding. He was complicated and frightening.

I couldn't choose between Moonie and Harry Babu that night, so I decided I'd give up pool until the Community House in Hopedale bought some pool tables, and only kids from Hopedale frequented them. It was a much safer place than either of the others, and it was a good place to meet if we weren't bowling.

But my safety came into question when I found out about "the tower" at the Community House and how a kid could make a reputation just by climbing that thing. It intrigued me.

Chapter Four
THINKING AHEAD

A FEW WEEKS BEFORE sophomore year began, I decided to climb the tower.

I had a plan, as always, and, as always, there were weak points in the plan. First, I would talk to the only person in town who had done it already and find out how he'd done it.

Over a game of eight ball at the Community House, I stood purposefully next to Mickey, the kid who had made his reputation climbing the tower last year. As we finished the game, I asked him, "So what's the big deal about this tower?"

Mickey lived in Hopedale but had been a tuition student at St. Mary's and in my class most of my life. He was a good kid.

"Why?" he asked, putting his cue back on the wall shelf.

"I thought I'd climb it, like you did."

"Have you seen the tower?" he asked.

"No, where is it?"

"Come on," he said. "Hey Buster, kid wants to see the tower. Can you give us a ride?"

Buster, only a few years older than us, had four fingers on one hand with a thumb, but only a thumb and one finger on the other. The others had been blown off when he had made a pipe bomb, which I guess had been a fad for a few years until a handful of kids, Buster being one of them, blew their hands off. The story told was that the first thing he did was hide his cigarettes from his mother so he wouldn't get in trouble, and then he cleaned up the blood, wrapped his hand in a towel, called Jimmy's Taxi, and went to the hospital.

He gave us a ride. He had a suicide knob on his steering wheel, which, in Buster's case, was more aptly named since he managed it with just one finger and his thumb.

The tower spoken of happened to be the water tower for the entire town. It stood probably a hundred and fifty to two hundred feet tall, and I estimated the diameter of the tank to be about forty or fifty feet. It was frightening, and I began to second guess my idea of climbing it.

"You climbed that?" I asked Mickey.

"Sure did," he said.

"How?"

He motioned me to follow him, and he took me to the further side where a metal ladder ascended, with the curved metal rungs welded into the side of the tank. I stared up along the rungs to the top. The iron steps blurred and shifted, elongating and seeming to climb all the way into the night sky.

"What's on top?"

"Well, there's a kind of cone-shaped roof that has a ball at the very tip."

"How big is the ball?" He thought for a few seconds and then decided, "It's bigger than a basketball, more like a medicine ball, but bigger and metal."

"What's the catch?" I asked. This didn't seem like more than climbing ladder a long way.

"You have to go up and touch the ball," Mickey said. "And you have to do it on the first try, and there's nothing to hang onto."

I turned around. It seemed that there wasn't only one car full of kids behind us. The car I'd ridden in had been followed. There were about fifteen other kids standing behind me, staring. They were waiting for me to chicken out, which would have been the rational thing to do, but would have afforded me an entirely different reputation from the one I had hoped for. I was, however, going on fourteen, in a new town, being watched closely by nearly every kid in town who was allowed out at night on their own. Rational flew out the window.

Without the surge of testosterone, I would never have put my foot on the first rung. But of course I did. It was just the beginning of one battle in the puberty wars into which I had just been drafted. This had a whole new set of rules. Being accepted by morons was more important than personal safety.

The beginning of the climb, the first fifty or seventy-five feet, ended before I knew it. I looked down to where the group had grown, and nearly everyone who had been at the Community House now stood at the bottom of the Hopedale Water Tower.

In the moonlight, all I could see from above were heads and shoulders and the occasional flair of a Zippo lighting a cigarette. Some of the smoke from below had reached me and set off an urge.

I hooked my arm under the rung in front of me, pulled a cigarette from my pack, fished into my pants for my lighter, and lit the cigarette. From below I heard someone in the distance say, "The crazy bastard is lighting a cigarette."

I guess I was a crazy bastard, so after a few puffs I tossed it down into the crowd who scattered to get away from the plummeting red tipped Kent.

What the hell am I doing? I asked myself, and a short, nervous laugh came out. The steel side of the tower loomed less than a foot away from my face, close enough so I could actually smell it.

One rung at a time, I climbed into the night. Finally, at the top, I pulled myself up and peered over the edge at the metal roof. I found it was cone shaped and constructed at about a forty-five-degree angle, and the ball on the top was not the size Mickey had described to me. A groove ran about a half-inch wide and fingertip deep. The groove circumnavigated the entire circumference of the roof about five feet up from the ladder. The rest of the cone consisted of slick metal, and it was a long way to the top.

Suddenly, it occurred to me. Mickey hadn't climbed to the top.

"No way," I said out loud. I realized what he had done. The ball was much bigger than he had said, and the metal was too slick to crawl up and too steep to walk up.

I climbed up over the lip and crawled to where I could hold on to the groove. I pulled up my feet so they couldn't be seen from below and laid motionless in terror. No one could see me from the ground, but there was no way in hell I was going to try to climb any farther. If I slipped, even from here, I would have to pray to God that I could grab the first rung of the ladder as I went over the top.

I lay motionless while I imagined myself climbing up the roof to the ball, touching the ball, and then crawling backwards to the ladder. When I was pretty sure I had imagined the timing right, I took a last glimpse of the night sky from my two-hundred -foot perch and said, "Hi God. Don't let me fall, alright?" I slid over the edge and back onto the ladder. I climbed down, shaking.

When I got to the ground, everyone surrounded me. I couldn't control my body and began to shiver with fright, inside and out. I was distracted since I could feel individual organs shivering; stomach, lungs, kidneys, each seemed to be shaking at its own frequency.

"It's cold up there," I said, and everyone laughed.

"Okay," Buster said. "How do we know he went to the top?"

It seemed there had been bets. Now stuff had to be proven. Mickey stepped up. "How big is the ball?" he asked.

I made believe I was measuring, my hands holding an expanding imaginary basketball. "A couple of feet in diameter, like the medicine ball at the gym. Maybe a little bigger," I said pointedly at Mickey, who nodded.

"How did you get to the top?" Mickey asked.

"There is a groove about five feet up. I used that." I turned quickly to the crowd. It was evident that they saw Mickey as sort of their prosecuting attorney, but I saw him for what he really was: my friend from a different life, a partner in crime. He knew what I was doing, and I knew what he hadn't done.

"He went to the top," Mickey said, affirming my ascent and my bona fide resume as a crazy bastard. Mickey's lie about me, and mine about him, weren't actually against the commandment that said we shouldn't bear false witness against our neighbor. It was sort of bearing false witness on behalf of our neighbors, him and me. There was, of course, the "thou shalt not lie" thing, but I thought, *For God's sake, one commandment at a time. I'm trying here.*

I had climbed the damn tower the same way Mickey had. Everybody cheered.

"What were you thinking?" Mike asked as the crowd thinned out, and we were walking to Buster's car, and I realized he hadn't bet on me to succeed.

"I kept thinking it would be a great time for the fifty-foot woman from that movie to show up." I turned to at Mike and held my hands out to both sides of my head with my thumbs and forefingers to create a large circle. "She had tits this big." We both laughed.

It is a great way to start my sophomore year of school as being the insane person who climbed the water tower and touched the ball on the first try. I hoped it would make up for my terrible fault of having spent my first thirteen years in places other than Hopedale.

On the way back to the center, someone handed me a GIQ of Narragansett Beer—the Giant Imperial Quart. I drank the whole thing. I guess I'd been accepted, at least by this crowd.

As I walked across the school lawn and into the front doors for my second year at General Draper High School, Principal Kent stood in the doorway welcoming kids. When he saw me, he just stared. He didn't take his eyes off me until I had passed him and tripped up the stairs to my old homeroom, where I got my new schedule, including my new homeroom.

Without meaning to, the school explained itself to me in the differences in courses my friends and I received.

There was no religion, no prayer in homeroom, but we were required to recite the Pledge of Allegiance. Those in the College Course were to learn English, ancient history, French (or Latin II), geometry, biology, wood shop, and gym. The business classes included shorthand, home economics, Spanish, earth science, and mechanical drawing. This last one was the tip off. It was a skill used best in the confines of "the factory." The General group had pretty much the same as the business group. The difference between them seemed to be that a lot of the school staff didn't seem to care if the "general" kids learned anything or not. I figured they were being groomed to fill in the lower positions in Diamond D's carpentry shop and foundry. Ironically, some of the smartest kids in the school were in the General Classes, and the ones who were best at taking the Iowa test were in the College Classes.

First, there was to be an assembly of the whole school. As we sat down in the auditorium, I saw the Great and Powerful Principal Kent up in the front of the room, waiting for the students to settle down.

"Something new," he shouted, and there was instant quiet. "This year, instead of paying your quarter at the lunch line, we will have lunch tickets." He held up a strip of tickets for us to see. "They will be bought in your homeroom, and you will need them in order to get your lunch."

He surveyed the assembly. "Now, in Milford, there is a Chinese laundry. When you drop off your shirt to be cleaned, they give you a ticket. When you go back to get your shirt, you need to present the China guy with the ticket, and as they say at the Chinese laundry, 'No tickee, no shirtee.'"

I had lived down the street from that laundry, and I knew that the people who owned it didn't talk like that. I wondered if anyone else thought this was just plain wrong to make fun of them just because they were Chinese. I saw very little evidence of displeasure. As a matter of fact, most people, including the majority of the teachers, smiled at his racist joke.

"So," the leader of our school continued. "Remember: no

tickee, no lunchee. Go to your homerooms."

My new homeroom was to be overseen by a woman from Milford who was about my father's age. I should have known there would be a problem.

I assessed her from my seat in the back of the room. She was a dark-skinned, southern Italian, with black hair, and although a bit heavy, I could see how she might have been attractive in her younger days. She checked her list of homeroom students, and at one point said, to herself, but out loud, "Oh no." She shook her head and repeated, "Oh no." She didn't say it as if shocked or scared, but with a determination not to let something happen. She closed the book, dropped it on the desk, and left the room. A few minutes later, she returned. She looked directly at me and beckoned with one finger. Again, I was back in the Wizard of Oz. I got up and walked, confused, to her desk.

"You are not in this homeroom," she said. "There has been a mistake."

Homeroom didn't matter to me, so I just said, "Okay, what homeroom am I in?"

"I don't care," she said, "but you are not here."

"So where should I go?"

"I don't care. Walk the halls until first period. Go to your first class. I don't care. You are just not here."

"Where am I supposed to get my tickee?" I asked.

"I don't care. Get out!"

I did, and from then on, I came to school late and went directly to my first class. A girl named Janet got me a ticket for lunch. It turned out she was the smartest kid in the class and also realized that the "tickee, shirtee" thing was just plain wrong.

That night at home when I told my mother what had happened, she told me, "You go tell this to your father," and she laughed.

My father laughed too when I told him the name of my new teacher.

"Mrs. Carpino," I told him, and he laughed.

"So she married Carpino, damn that's funny," he said to my mother.

It seemed there had been some kind of interplay between them, and she came away not liking my father at all, and again, I paid for what he had done in high school as I had paid a bit for him punching a nun when he had attended St. Mary's. I mean, he was perfectly right in the nun thing since she had opened the door and thrown a baseball at him while he sat in class and the baseball hit him in the head. It was explained to me that he had made an error in a crucial game while playing first base, and she was his payback unless he made an immaculate reception… which he didn't and got hit in the head. She also went on to shove a few kids down the stairway for real or imagined slights of the religion, but I had no idea what he had done to this new woman when they were kids. He might have been right. He might have been wrong, but as sure as shooting, I was the one who was going to pay for it. The sins of the father and all.

It was, however, also in my second year in Hopedale that

I found the Catholic Church in town. Strangely, the parish chose the same name as the Italian Church in Milford, Sacred Heart. One afternoon, Cecelia mentioned that her family had gone to the Sacred Heart Church.

I asked why she and her family went all the way to Milford for Mass at the Italian church, and she said it was the name of the church in Hopedale too, and it occurred to me that, just because I didn't live in Milford didn't mean I shouldn't go to church.

So that Sunday, I walked the three miles to church. I sat in the middle row, mostly because there were high school girls in the row in front of me. One of them was very well endowed and when we all got to say the Pledge of Allegiance in school, we watched her, because when she put her hand on her heart she missed by a few inches, and we could dream.

The Mass began, but before we made it to the Mass of the Faithful, the priest halted. He simply stopped speaking the Mass as a woman and two men walked into the church.

She was a stately, gray-haired woman, and the two men were much younger. As they ushered her into a pew only a few behind me, the priest smiled and began to speak again. "I suppose you all know Mrs. Draper, but what you might not know is that without her, we wouldn't have a church here in Hopedale. So I welcome her to this, her first Mass here in town."

From the murmur that crawled throughout the church, it became apparent that it hadn't been common knowledge about the church or that a Draper dared to be a Catholic.

The priest continued, "Mrs. Draper, with your permission?"

I looked back at her. He spoke for God and asked her for permission. *Now that is power*, I thought. She nodded, and he continued. "It was Mrs. Draper who made a transaction with Father Cuddihy in Milford so many years ago to allow a Catholic church to be built on some land she owned here. Until then, all attempts to build a Catholic church in Hopedale had failed."

I heard later that, in response, the good father was to allow the Draper family to purchase a building near the Irish church in Milford. The building was owned by St. Mary's diocese, and the corporation wanted to buy it so a competitor, who had a process for making elastic wear, wouldn't be allowed to set up shop there.

The priest returned to the Mass.

That afternoon Richard Millen, a friend from school, said he had a job cleaning up after a party at the Rod and Gun Club, and he needed to get a handful of friends to help him. I was happy to have been asked. So, notwithstanding the commandment about keeping the Sabbath holy, I agreed to help him. I could use the money.

We all went up in Buster's car: Mike, Peter, Screwhead, Mammal and Pancho, and, of course, Millen and Buster. We were a walking heresy.

A stag party had occurred the night before, and the place reeked of beer and processed beer. As Millen told me when I asked about the smell, "You don't buy beer. You just rent it."

As we began cleaning, I found a bottle that hadn't been opened, so I rented it. By the time we had the place clean, we had found the key to the cooler, and we were all drunk.

I sat on the porch with Millen, Mike, and Peter. We drank and smoked Peter's mother's cigarettes. When we finished, we drove around for a while. It felt good to be a part of this group; the group of lost boys who Hopedale didn't want around. Then, when most of the others went home, I asked Buster to give me a ride to my sister Diane's house. Diane was seventeen and married with a kid on the way. I figured I could visit until I became sober enough to go home.

Chapter Five
YOUNG LOVE

DIANE HAD RETURNED TO Milford to begin her married life. She had married a seventeen-year-old kid who worked as a bagger at the supermarket, played passable rock and roll drums, danced real good, and didn't drink alcohol. But he was an Italian.

In Milford, the Irish and Italians were supposed to be mortal enemies. My father called them WOPs, an acronym often stamped on the luggage of the immigrants at Ellis Island. It meant the bag belonged to someone who had entered the country Without a Passport. Of course, two of his best friends, Mario and Davey, were both Italians, and our neighbors, the Trottas, were some of my mother's favorite people. So there was that quandary to figure out, especially for the twins, who were now working in a predominantly Italian shoe shop. Sheila had quieted herself into anonymity, but on her first day in the shop, Nancy made a name for herself. On St. Patty's Day, and as a joke, Nancy had dressed up as a leprechaun. She had the hat, the green-suspendered shorts, the black shoes and white socks, and when my father had sent word that she had gotten the job, she went… without changing a thing. She walked into the dingy, dirt laden room of the shop where she would be working, into the midst of the paesanos who populated the shop workforce, dressed as the symbol of Ireland. She didn't actually want the job. She wanted to be in school.

Diane and Joe had married against the wishes of his parents and Father Manahan, who, after a talk with my father, agreed to marry them. I guess if they got married, what they had been doing wouldn't be considered adultery anymore. Dad did a lot of things wrong, but at the drop of a hat, he would go to war for his family or friends if he thought they were being treated unfairly. He had always told us how we Hourihans were the descendants of warriors, "the protectors of the kings of Ireland," and therefore we were warriors ourselves. I, in turn, had always thought he should feed us more if he wanted us to be big enough to be effective warriors.

Diane was seventeen, married, and pregnant. I guess Dad figured he wouldn't like her getting rid of the kid, and he didn't want to have a single mother living with him, and if Joe could get her in a family way, he could damn well step up and do the right thing. There was no shotgun involved only because Scrapper Jack didn't need a shotgun to make people do what he wanted, and what he wanted was for these two stupid, over-hormoned kids to enter the holy sacrament of marriage and get everything right with the Catholic God. I guess the good Father Manahan saw it that way too.

I hopped out of Buster's car in front of her house and begged him not to burn out when he left. He did it anyway.

The driveway was dark, and I had had a bit to drink, so I stumbled a little before getting to the side door.

I knocked and heard my sister, who for a while had also been my mother in the Arizona desert until the second half of my family arrived, and she became my sister again. I think that insane duality wore on her every day.

I squinted as I stepped from the darkness of the side porch into the blazing incandescent light of the kitchen.

"You've been drinking," she said, peeking at me sideways and for only a few seconds. We could always tell, having been raised on the need to know immediately if someone entering our home was drunk.

"A little," I answered.

"Sit down," she said, and she put on some water for coffee. "How's that new school?"

"Okay, I guess. Where's Joe?"

"Work. He'll be home any minute." Headlights flashed across the windows as she spoke, and she added, "Here he is now."

It took him a few minutes to park the '49 baby blue Ford, lock it up, and get to the door.

As he stepped inside the kitchen, Diane was placing a cup of instant coffee on the table in front of me. I watched the grounds cling to the sides of the cup as if they were fending off drowning.

Joe went directly to the bread box and took out a small loaf of Italian bread. He asked Diane, "Did you get this at Mazzarelli's?"

"I did," she answered.

I watched with interest as he began collecting things from the cupboard. He pulled out the olive oil, checked the label, nodded, and then reached for the red wine vinegar. He reached into the fridge and took out a tomato, the lettuce, and an onion. He foraged for a second or two and then asked, "Isn't there any provolone?"

I wondered why he didn't pronounce the final "e."

I checked silently with my sister to see if there was, in fact, any provolone.

"It's in the top," she said.

He found it.

"Where's the cold cuts?" he asked

"Right there in front of you. If it was a snake, it would 'a bit you."

He couldn't find it, which was strange since I could see a package of bologna and one of salami right in front of him. He almost had his hand on top of it.

"There's no prosciutto?"

He pronounced it Pasoot. And in my half-sober state, I heard "soup."

"No. It was too expensive."

"Damn," he shouted. Joe allowed himself this one swear word but that was the only one.

I have to explain. Joe was not a bad guy. Actually, he was a pretty good kid trying his best to use the examples of his father and a host of other Milford Italians to form his own husband self. Now, those examples consisted of some bad and some good. It seemed to me he was an imitation of the head of the family, the capo famiglia, and therefore the boss, and he wanted Diane to be the barefoot, pregnant wife, the moglie asservita, who was supposed to have soup and sandwich ready for him when he got home from work. I tried to hide my smile because that was never going to happen. I sipped my coffee and watched him.

"How can I have a sandwich after work if there's no pasoot? All I ask is that you have some dinner for me when I get home. Can't you do that?" he shouted.

Diane observed him through squinted eyes, and I wondered if he had a death wish.

What sounded like a domestic problem, from where I sat, was just an Italian kid trying to be the man of the family by complaining that he didn't have a sandwich and soup for his dinner. He was supposedly putting his subservient wife in her place, but my Irish sister was subservient to no one.

I walked to the cupboard and took a can of tomato soup from the shelf.

"Hey, Joe," I said. "Calm down. There's soup right here." I handed the can to him and went back to my chair at the table and began drinking my coffee again.

"Soup?" he shouted, near hysterical. "Soup? I don't want any soup. I want some pasoot for a sandwich." He shook his head. "I have the right bread from Mazzarelli's, some tomato, lettuce, onion, some provolone, olive oil, and vinegar, and if I had some pasoot I could build a sandwich."

"What the hell is pasoot?" I laughed.

"It's meat!" he shouted.

Diane and I smiled a little.

"Oh, sorry. I thought you were losing your mind because you wanted some soup."

Joe was one of those good kids who just couldn't be scary, even while shouting "pasoot" at the top of his lungs. I didn't think I had to step in or do anything. As a matter of fact, I had faith that Diane could take him if it came to that, but an idea popped into my head.

"Joe, it's only six o'clock. You know what you do have? You have a car. Go buy some damn prasoup then you can have your sandwich."

He wanted to slam something down on the counter in disgust. He stood there, holding only the tomato.

"You're going to have to clean that up when you get back," Diane said.

Joe reached for his keys.

"Hey," I said.

"What?" he shouted.

"Can I grab a ride home?"

He nodded and headed for the door.

I finished my coffee, thanked Diane, and caught up with my new brother-in-law.

The ride toward home was quiet. I thought, *Maybe they were too young to get married.*

On the drive, I thought about their situation and came

to the conclusion that it's easy to choose between good and evil; easy to choose between good and good. It's choosing between bad and worse that has always been our dilemma. Maybe sacraments aren't always a good thing.

Millen refused to get thrown out of school with the rest of us back during the cornfield thing, so we made him pay by convincing his mother he wanted us to "customize" his '53 Plymouth coupe that sat in his driveway during school.

So anyway, the cornfield thing.

The night I left my sister's place and got a ride with Joe, who decided to go shopping for some prasoot to build a sandwich, I got dropped off downtown instead of having him drive me home.

A group of us were sitting in cars on the one-way street when Millen came limping into town in his maroon three-on-the-post Plymouth. With corn stalks hanging off every unprotected metal edge, his car looked like the scarecrow from Oz.

He convinced everyone to drive up through a neighboring town and into this cornfield, where we made a circle in the center by driving around and around until all the stalks were flat or torn up.

I think it was probably the first crop circle.

We wouldn't have gone with him if we only had a brain, but there we were. Five cars, about twenty-five kids, and we raced. And no one could even see us from the road. We were hidden by the untouched seven-foot corn stalks around the edges of the field.

We all got caught, except for Millen. It turns out cars make noise.

We got tossed out of school, and our parents each had to pay a whole lot of money to the guy who owned the farm. It seems we had destroyed most of his crop, so now he couldn't sell it to markets, or feed his cows, or pay his bills.

This meant he was going to get the entire annual payoff from our parents. Then he could sell the remaining corn and make out better this year than any other year.

The fact that our parents didn't do anything wrong yet got overcharged didn't seem to bother him. I guess the false god of money made everything okay. The only thing that might have stopped him from overcharging might have been a belief in God, but here, that didn't seem to be an alternative.

As for us kids, we hadn't known we could get suspended from school for something we did outside school. By Monday, we knew.

Millen was the only one who didn't get caught, so he didn't get suspended. While he was in school, we hacksawed the top off his car, nailed an alarm clock to his dashboard (tachometer), tied a pillow to his trunk with belts (parachute), nosed it, decked it, and threw away the hub caps. Then Dee Joe painted flames on the hood and the fenders.

He should have gotten thrown out for a week so we would have a ride, but he didn't, so he got a totally new kind of car. A roadster, I think.

Rules just kept continuing to blur, and this fog made it very difficult to turn over a new leaf, but I had promised my mother, and I was going to try. As my father would say, "Come hell or high water."

Chapter Six
A LITTLE GOOD GOES A LONG WAY

*T*HAT COLD FALL DAY came with torrential rains, but we took refuge in the stairwell inside the building after school while waiting for the bus home.

A kid with an umbrella stood outside the front door of the school and let the rest of us know when a bus arrived. Everyone who took the South Hopedale bus stood on the stairs just inside the front door, keeping dry.

Jane stood across from me, a short brunette who was considered one of the most attractive girls in the freshman class. I had to agree.

An older kid named Phil Zuzi loomed over her, harassing her.

"Five bucks," he said. He stood on the top step, leering down at her as she tried to shrink into herself a few steps below him.

She clutched her books close to her chest, her gaze

averted from his. She didn't answer him.

"Come on," he said again. "Five bucks, you take off just your blouse and bra. You don't have to do it here. We can go out in someone's car."

"No," she said, and stared at the floor.

"Fine," Phil said. "How about ten bucks, and you take off everything?"

"No," she said again.

I knew I would have loved to see that and started paying closer attention to what he was offering.

"Okay," he said. "Fifteen bucks, you show everything."

I didn't like the way she looked. This wasn't funny. Jane remained frightened and alone, with no friends in sight. She couldn't raise her eyes from the floor, and I could almost feel her willing the bus to arrive.

Phil smiled a half-smile and leaned closer to her. "Twenty bucks. That's my best offer."

I crossed to the other side and stepped onto the stair between them. "Knock it off, Phil," I said.

He tried to push me aside. "What? Get out of the way."

"No," I said. I knew I had told my mother I wouldn't get in fights anymore, but I couldn't let this happen. I had been frightened and alone before, and I was pretty sure this came under the heading of not coveting stuff.

"You got a problem with naked girls?" he asked.

I turned for a second to Jane, and she looked back. She didn't lift her head, just her eyes. They were usually a bright blue but were dim today. "No," I said. "I would love to see Jane naked, but she said 'No.'"

"Big deal," the older boy said and started to push by me.

I reached out and grabbed his shirt. "It is a big deal. You got a right to ask, but she's got a right to say, 'No.' And she said 'No,' so knock it off."

"Asshole," he said just as the kid with the umbrella stepped inside and said, "South Hopedale is here."

Jane pushed by both of us and stepped out into the rain.

I followed her, and we both headed for the bus.

She didn't say anything to me or even nod. She sat in the back of the bus, but at her stop, as she walked by me on her way to the door, she rested her hand on my shoulder for just a second as she passed, and I knew I had done the right thing.

It felt good, even though I sure would have liked to see her naked.

By the middle of the year, French class had become a hoot, since the teacher, Mrs. Carpino, was the same teacher who had refused to have me in home room. This time, she lost the battle with the guidance department. Placed in the college track, which included a language, I was to learn French. It was the way of Hopedale. Business students and Generals learned Spanish. College learned French. I was in the College course. The god of the Iowa test had put me there, and she could do nothing about it. She mostly avoided eye contact, probably trying to convince herself I did not exist. She never took attendance, and I believed by doing this she would not have to acknowledge my presence. So when she called on me one day about halfway through the year, I had not been listening and, therefore, paid no attention to her question.

"Mr. Hourihan," she said louder.

"Yes?"

"I asked you how you say this word."

She pointed at the broach she wore on her formidable chest. I knew our vocabulary lesson for last night had the world broach in the list.

I knew the French word, since it sounded the same as the English word, but I also knew her intent: to make a fool of me for the same reason. Broach translated was Broche and was pretty much pronounced the same way.

She now had walked right up to my desk and bent over in front of me, pointing at the broach.

"Translate!" she said.

I inspected down the front of her low-cut dress top and smiled.

"I'm pretty sure we don't know the word for those, Mrs. Carpino."

It took her a second, but she then realized what I had meant.

"Get out!" she shouted, her face beet red all the way down to her broche and beyond.

She tried to slap me, but I ducked, got up quickly, and left. At the door, I waved goodbye and went to art class. Nothing else happened.

Of course she gave me a D in French, and with a B in English, a C in history, and a C in geometry, I needed to do something about my report card.

A week before report cards were to be sent out, I skipped a study period and went to the guidance office.

"I need to get out of the College Course," I told Mr. Brickly.

"Why?"

"Well, I guess because I don't want to go to college, and my parents wouldn't have the money to pay for it if I did."

He got up. "Just a minute," he said and went into the next room. I figured he decided to look up my Iowa tests again.

I saw something on a table that caught my eye. This year being the onset of computer-generated forms, a pile of continuous-feed blank report cards sat on the table. Next to them was a stack of "official" envelopes with the name of the school at the return address spot. Without a second thought, I grabbed an envelope and tore off one of the report cards at the perforation. I slid them both into my biology book. It may have been the first time I had opened the book that year.

He returned and said, "I'm sorry, John. We can't do it this year. Maybe we can get it done next year."

I agreed and quickly left the room.

That afternoon, I snuck into the empty typing classroom.

I typed my address on the envelope and then rolled the report card into the typewriter.

"Let's see," I said to no one. "I think I deserve a B in English." I typed. "And a B in biology." I typed. I gave myself a B in geometry and a B in history, an A in gym, and a B in French.

Now all I had to do was intercept the real report card when they mailed it to my house and replace it with this one. A few weeks later, I did just that.

I told myself it actually changed nothing in my permanent record, but it would be better for my parents to think their kid was doing well in school. It was, of course, a rationalization, but now, because of events in my home life, my school life, and my social life, I realized there was always more than one truth. I was getting pretty good at rationalizing stuff.

For instance, I got a job picking apples in Mendon after school to make enough money for beer and cigarettes. It was better than stealing the money, I rationalized, and since in many countries it was perfectly legal for someone my age to drink beer, I wasn't really doing anything wrong there either. It wasn't a case of right and wrong. It was just a case of geography.

On a mid-summer Friday night, riding around in Millen's car and drinking with some friends, I started telling jokes, and Geno didn't like the Italian ones.

"If you tell one more Italian joke, I'm going to break your head," he said.

We were both in the back seat with another Irish kid, and the guys in the front were laughing, so I said, "Why do Italians have sloped foreheads?"

"Why?" someone in the front asked.

"Because whatever question you ask them, they don't know the answer, and they slap their forehead, like this."

"Stop the car," Geno demanded.

"Okay, slope head, let's do it," I answered. I laughed. He didn't.

Geno weighed fifty pounds more than me, and all of us assumed that he'd be true to his word. He was going to kick my ass.

As we all began to exit the car for the big fight, my Irish friend said, "I can get you out of this if you want."

"Nope," I said. "I have an idea."

It only took a few seconds for Geno to grab me in a headlock and pull me to the ground. I punched him in the ear. He tightened his grip. I punched him again in the ear, then I punched him several times in the same ear, and then I said, "Okay. I give up. You're too strong for me. I give up."

Geno let go of my head. His ear was red and swollen. We began to climb into the back seat of the car. Nothing on me hurt. Nothing was bruised. I hadn't been hit anywhere. My hair wasn't even messed up. His ear grew nearly three times the size it had been before he got out of the car, and now we were getting back into the car, and because I said, "I give up," he thought he had won. No one laughed out loud because Geno didn't seem to know it had been my last joke of the night.

Chapter Seven
THE RULES OF THE ROAD

AS I BEGAN MY junior year in Hopedale, my family was on the eve of destruction, and life decisions were getting more and more serious.

My father's drinking fog was progressing and acquiring a firm grip on his everyday life. When he had been drinking only on weekends, he was a great guy for five days a week. Now the tide had reversed. My mother was getting closer and closer to her sister, who lived in Maine. I thought that at any minute, she might bolt and go live there. The girls were all searching for marriage partners to get out of the house, and the twins and my father had taken jobs in the clock factory down the road in Ashland. Dennis was becoming a true introvert lost in his music, but Neil was quietly becoming an integral part of Hopedale's next powerhouse baseball team.

It seemed to me that his little league all-star team never lost. In Hopedale, if your team never lost, everyone knew your name, in a good way. I guess I was just a day late. I had tried to get onto the high school baseball team but had been told by the coach, "Get a damn haircut," and I never returned. He never even gave me a tryout. I was told the team had been picked when they were in grade school. I was pretty sure Mr. Kent had a hand in my treatment by the baseball coach. It seemed there wasn't a spot on the team: You know, infield, outfield, catcher, Irish Milford punk. It was just not in the cards for a few more years at least.

In October, I had turned seventeen. Everything took a back seat to my will to get my driver's license. I carried the RMV rules book with me everywhere I went, but no matter how many rules 1 learned, I couldn't manage the coordination I needed to find the friction point of a clutch on a hill to keep the driver education car from rolling backwards. Of course, then as I gunned it and popped the clutch, the tires would burn. The teacher was a nice lady with an incredible amount of patience. Even with her calm demeanor, she would get seriously pissed that everyone on the street would turn to see whose car was burning out, and they would see the sign that said, "Jenny's Driving School" and laugh.

The best part of learning to drive, though, was I took my

lessons with Jane. I would sometimes get a ride home with her and her family, which was great. She smelled incredibly good.

One night, however, when her family was going out to eat, I had to thumb home. I had hung out downtown for a while, and then decided to head home. On the trip I was handed the incentive I needed to get more coordinated.

I was thumbing down Route 140 from downtown. I was about four miles from the house when a white Cadillac stopped to give me a ride.

I trotted up to the car and opened the passenger side door.

"Where you headed?" the middle-aged man asked.

He was thin and balding and wore a royal blue suit. Since it was about nine at night, I figured he was heading home late from work.

"Mellen Street," I said.

"No problem. Get in." He smiled.

The interior of the car was immaculate. Not a gum wrapper, not a store receipt, not a speck of dirt on the floor.

"Going home?" he asked.

"Right," I answered.

"You live on Mellen Street?"

"Right."

There was a pause, and then he said, "So, you go to Hopedale High School?"

"Yes," I answered.

"I know some girls who go to Hopedale High School."

I thought that was strange.

"Me too," I said.

"You got a girlfriend?" he asked.

"What?"

"You got a girlfriend?"

"No."

He reached over to the radio and turned it on. As he finished fiddling with the knob, he let his hand drop onto my knee.

I had heard about this type of thing, guys who liked guys. It sounded a little weird to me, but I figured I had better make a decision pretty quick.

"Is this okay?" he asked.

"Well actually, no," I said, brushing his hand away. "No, I like girls."

We were at Mellen Street, and I asked him to stop. "I live right up here," I said.

He pulled to the curb. I began to get out of the car. He seemed to be intently listening to the radio. "Are you going to tell anyone about this?" he asked without looking at me.

I stopped, half in and half out of the car.

I thought, *He's just a guy. If I tell my father, he is going to get beat up. If I tell the cops, he is going to get arrested.* I didn't think he deserved either of those alternatives. I made my decision.

"No," I said. "I don't see how anything good could come of that."

"Thank you," he said.

I got out, and he drove away.

As I walked to the house, I thought, *I really have to get that license.*

I never told anyone about it. I felt worried for this guy. Someone was going to tell someone, and it wouldn't be good for him. A few days later, it occurred to me that if God made us all in his image, then this guy who had picked me up was made in God's image too. I saw him one more time when I thumbed a ride home. I saw the Caddy coming in the dusk of Route 140. I stopped thumbing and turned my back to the oncoming car and walked. As he passed by, he beeped the horn and waved. I waved back. I guess, in a strange way, I had made a friend who I would never see again. *Decisions in my life are getting more and more important*, I thought.

School droned on, but there was a new English teacher who I found interesting. She walked into the class and wrote on the board. Every teacher had done this, but instead of her name in the corner of the board, she took the entire board and wrote in three-foot letters, L-S-D. Then in smaller letters she chalked, Lysergic Acid Diethylamide.

"You don't have to know the words written small," she said, "but you better know about the three large letters."

She stalked across the front of the room. She was very tall, not skinny, but tall, and she had short brown hair and kind eyes. She wore a tweed-like gray suit, and when she turned sideways, I could see her pack of Marlboros inside her top, most likely stuck inside her bra. I was about to laugh when she began talking again.

"LSD is coming. You may not have heard of it yet, but it will be here soon, and you will all know what it is."

She stopped walking, turned to us, and shouted, "Stay the hell away from it! It will screw up your life."

She went on a rant, telling us how people in Russia first used this drug, and then how the CIA got hold of it and used it on people without their knowing anything about what it would do.

"Some of them went crazy, one guy killed himself. He jumped out of a hotel window. No matter what anyone tells you about LSD…" Again, she turned to us and shouted, "Stay the hell away from it!"

Done with shocking the hell out of us, she erased the board and wrote her name.

"Mrs. Marion."

The class was still in shock when I raised my hand.

"Yes," she said.

"Are you married to a doctor?"

The whole class turned to my seemingly stupid question.

"Yes, why do you ask?"

"Because when I was a kid, I got dragged hanging from the bumper of a delivery truck. I was in the first grade. This doctor, Dr. Marion, came to my house and worked on my knees, and I wasn't supposed to walk again, but because of him, I did. I just wanted to say thank you. I never got a chance to thank him, for me walking and all. Could you tell him thank you from John Hourihan?"

Her eyes watered. "I will," she said.

"He may not remember me. I lived up on Purchase Street in Milford."

She turned her kind eyes to me and evenly said, "He remembers you, John. I'll tell him what you said."

She became one of the most loved teachers in the school, by everyone but a few of the other teachers. I think she was too honest for some of them.

The memories of first grade, the nuns, the church, the priest, came back with the re-emergence of the name of Dr. Marion, and they made me think about how I had been stealing money from a small store run by a kind elderly man in the center of town and rationalizing it. The rules of St. Mary's rushed back to me as I walked down the hallway of this noticeably Protestant school. The stealing was wrong. No rationalization could make it right. I didn't need Catholic rules to tell me I'd done something wrong. I knew it in my bones. I noticed a note on the bulletin board outside the guidance office, and I stopped to read it. It said there was a job in a bowling alley in Mendon as a pinsetter. I coaxed a ride from a friend after school and walked into the alleys in the cellar of a building in the center of the adjacent town of Mendon. A few minutes later I had a job, ten cents a string.

I told my sister Patty what was going on at my job, and I told her I had a problem with it. She told me it was because I had a brain, and something about this "avoidance-avoidance-conflict" thing. I was a pinsetter. I had been for a week or so. It was before the machines. When I took the job, no one told me the rest of the pinsetters, who were all from out of town, were like cartoons. I was sure they were normal people outside the alley, but when they came to work, they were not like people at all. What I was explaining to Patty was a questionable activity called the cigarette game. Just a few days with Larry, Big Meggy, Davey Dave, and Mel, and I was having visions of Pinocchio being surrounded by the likes of J. Worthington Foulfellow while trying to become a real boy. Big Meggy was, well, big. At sixteen years old, he was a full six foot four with a black Fred Flintstone mop, weighed at least twice as much as I did, and seemed within the confines of the alleys to sport half the IQ of a mollusk. Larry was skinny, my size, with a face twisted by a hard birth, tiny green eyes, sparse blond hair like a baby chicken, and a crooked laugh. At seventeen, Davey Dave was a small, bald boy with a big head full of bruises and bumps, a phrenologist's dream. And Mel was an over-dressed, slicked and oiled black DA hairdo, collar up, camels in the sleeve, bona fide 1950's juvenile delinquent with a gold tooth. Cartoons.

We were paid ten cents a string to climb on a perch between two alleys right beside the pins, wait for the ball to go rumbling through, and scatter the wooden missiles everywhere. Then we'd jump down and pull out the Ten-Pin dead wood or reset the pins. Candlepins were the worst because the pins would spin through the air and hit you a lot.

Davey wore a football helmet to protect his head. It didn't work. On Fridays, the pin boys would put up a few bucks of their pay, and three strings later, someone took all the money. The first time I won, Mel told me about the cigarette game. We each stood at the end of our alley, faced off, extended our right arms and placed them firmly on the pit perch so my fist was beside his elbow and vice versa.

Meggy lit a Tareyton and wedged it, filter first, between our arms about half-way up. Whoever moved first would lose. It would continue until there was a winner or the cigarette went out. At first it was easy. You could feel the warmth and still act cool.

We stared into each other's eyes. I noticed there was nothing behind Mel's eyes at all. There was no sense of a single synapse, just vacant space. Slowly we started feeling the heat, but no one moved. It got a little worse, and we started to sweat. Then it began hurting. A few seconds longer and you could smell the hair on your arm burning.

Then came the smell of burning flesh. But still we remained stock-still.

This is the avoidance-avoidance conflict my sister told me about. If you moved, it was a bad thing. You wanted to avoid people laughing at you and the loss of twelve bucks. But if you didn't move, your skin started melting and blistering, and you wanted to avoid this too. Avoidance-Avoidance. It sometimes makes you do absolutely nothing.

I remember pulling my arm away when the sting turned to fire shooting up my arm. I stared into Mel's face and shouted, "What the hell is wrong with you! Are you insane? This isn't a game. This is stupidity. Why would you do this to yourself for a few bucks?" Since Mel was my ride home, I got to walk home that night, about twelve miles through the woods. That is, of course, another thing you might want to avoid. I felt it was time for a change. Within a week, I quit that job.

Chapter Eight
A LICENSE TO DRIVE

*M*Y LIFE HAD BECOME drinking beer, taunting the police, riding around with drunk drivers, getting in or watching fights, trying to just barely pass high school classes without studying, and trying my best to keep it all from my parents. I needed something to stabilize my life. I needed to grow up.

I made a decision. I would get my license, and then I would get a girlfriend. It seemed to work for others. I thought I would give it a shot. How hard could it be?

The day of the road test, we showed up at the registry office in Milford. There were three of us: myself, Jane, and Marty, one of the guys who had blown off his hand. We drove the same course we had driven every week for two months with our driving instructor, Jenny. We drove along Main Street, took a hard left, and went up the street to the stop sign at the top of the hill. There we stopped, pulled up the emergency brake, and then, finding the friction point on the clutch, we would hold the car still on the hill. We then unleashed the brake and drove back down Main Street and out to Route 140. By the time I got there, the registry officer said, "Okay, John, go ahead back to the registry." Either I was really good, or he was really frightened.

Jenny went into the office while we waited in the car. She came out and handed Marty his temporary license. "Good job," she said.

She handed one to Jane. "You were perfect," she said.

"John," she said, "How the hell you ever got a license, I don't know. You frighten me. Please don't drive in Milford, okay?" I smiled and reached for the license.

"I mean it," she said and held onto the paper. "Not in Milford, okay?"

Later she told my father that I probably got it because the Registrar of Massachusetts had a name fortunate for me, William Hourihan. I saw his signature on my license and asked Dad about it.

"He might be related." he said to me, "but I don't know him. Second cousin or something."

Next, I had to figure out how to get a girlfriend.

I set my sights on Cecelia, my neighbor. She was smart, friendly, and one of the cool girls at school.

I had no idea how to treat girls. My initial idea of a date was to buy a six-pack and ask if someone wanted to go to the woods and help me drink it. How could she say no? I lived next door, and the day I helped her get into the shed in the back through the window, I had pushed her up by putting both hands on her ass and shoving. She had turned back at me for a second but then ignored it. I figured that we had made a connection.

I had a plan. As always, my plan had a flaw or two.

I told my sister Sheila part of my plan was on a Friday night to let her have the family car we shared. Sheila liked that part.

"Who are you going to ask out?" she asked.

"Cecelia," I said.

Sheila laughed.

"What are you laughing at?"

"Do you even know what a date is?" she asked, still laughing.

"I ask her out, and if she says yes, I buy a six-pack."

"No!" Sheila said. "No. You find a place to go, like a movie or a restaurant or a dance, and you take her there. You pay. You treat her nice, and you bring her home. That's a date. A six pack? Are you kidding me?"

"Okay," I said. "I'll do that. Where should I go?"

"You're in luck," she said. "I have two extra tickets to a play in Milford. It's in a couple of weeks. I'm going with friends. You can ask her, and if she says yes, I can drive you."

With the two tickets in my pocket, I called Cecelia and asked if I could get a ride to the Friday dance at the Town Hall in Hopedale. She said her friend's mother was driving them so I could go with them too.

I was so nervous, I didn't even look at her at the dance.

I stood with my friends, fidgeting and killing time until the last dance. I went outside to wait for my ride home. I planned to ask her when we got out of the car at her house. I had it all figured out. We lived next door to each other, so I would get out when she did, and then I would ask her out.

The ride only lasted about ten minutes. I was struck mute. Then something unexpected happened. Just before the car stopped, with us both sitting next to each other in the back seat, Cecelia put her hand on mine. She looked at me, leaned over a little, and whispered, "When we get out, can I talk to you?"

"Okay," I said.

We stepped out of the car into the night in front of our two houses. I tried to calm my heartbeat so she wouldn't hear it. The car being driven by our friend's mother drove off into the darkness and up the hill. The tickets were burning a hole in my pocket.

I leaned against the rail fence to my house and waited, trying to be cool, hoping my heart would stop pounding, and my armpits would stop sweating. This was even better than I had expected.

"I need to ask you a favor," she said.

"Sure," I answered.

"Could you get me a date with Richard?"

I was crushed. Not only was my plan totally destroyed by this one short sentence, but Richard was a good friend, and I couldn't even lie and tell her he wouldn't want to go out with her.

Or could I?

"Sure," I said. "I can do that."

"Thank you," she said and turned and walked to her house.

I spent the night weighing the alternatives.

I could tell him nothing and report back to her that he didn't like her. That would hurt her, though, and I didn't want to do that.

I could tell him she really didn't like him at all, and he wouldn't ask her out.

Then I thought about something else.

One of the smart girls in the class had been told by her doctor that her feet were growing wrong, and she would have to wear nurses' shoes for a few years. The nurses' shoes were big, clunky white things that stuck out when a girl wore a skirt and nylons. The girl spent a few days at home crying. She couldn't face her peers, who already didn't like that she was not only a smart girl but a really pretty one to boot. For a teenager, embarrassment in school was worse than a death penalty.

On the first day she had worn them to school, among the twitters and behind-the-back laughing, Richard had asked her why she would wear such a fashion no-no.

She told him about the doctor and the feet, and he said, "Don't worry. I'll take care of it."

Richard was popular, good looking, athletic, and a decent person. In our school, acceptability depended on his imprimatur.

The following day, Richard and a few friends wore white bucks to school. White bucks had been out of fashion for a decade, having died with the flame-out that was Pat Boone, but now, because of Richard, in our school they were back in, and they were almost exactly like nurses' shoes. He had just saved his classmate a year of self-conscious teen angst.

I had to just tell him.

The next day, I told Richard that he should ask Cecelia out.

"No," he said unexpectedly.

"No? Are you shitting me? Why not?"

"Look at her, man, she's not someone who goes out with me. She's out of my league."

He started to walk away. In my heart, I wanted so much to just let it happen. Go back and tell Cecelia, "He said no."

I heard myself say, "You're right, Dick. There's no way she would go out with you. Sorry I bothered you." That is of course what I said in my head, but it never reached my mouth.

"Dick, you know I live right next door to her, right?"

He turned back. "Right."

"You know we're friends, right?"

"Right."

"You know we talk to each other, right?"

His eyes widened, showing interest. "Right."

"I guarantee you, if you ask her out, she will not turn you down. You won't be embarrassed."

Being turned down by a girl was the main fear of every teenage boy who fought the effects of hormones, coupled with a good supply of normal teenage self-loathing. A punch in the face hurt less than a girl saying, "I have to visit my grandmother that night," or, "I'm sorry, that's the night I have to wash my hair."

Within a week, they were going steady, and I had to make a new plan.

Again, I found myself sitting on my front steps in the darkness. Inside, the TV blared. My mother stayed up to watch the new nighttime show. The new host, Johnny Carson, was funny. I almost went inside, but my mind started to wonder.

It occurred to me that I didn't know where I belonged.

I was fighting the first battles of the puberty wars with a bunch of people I didn't know. Not that long ago, I had considered myself to be a reluctant soldier of Jesus. I believed in the Apostles' Creed and the Ten Commandments and the golden rule, even though I didn't go by the rules all the time.

I had never belonged to any group I had been a part of. I never felt better or worse than them — just forever different. God and the church had given me a lot of rules, but to follow them always, without first determining the best options for my own safety, was just dumb. I had told the truth in this new school and been punished for it, and I watched a priest during a Mass defer to the woman whose family ran the factory in town.

The Bible said that it was wrong, that it was a sin, for a guy to be queer. It was right there in the Holy Book, but that was written by men, not God. It was written by Paul and Leviticus, and I didn't know either of them. Jesus talked about thousands of things that He said were a sin, but He never said it was a sin to love someone of your own sex. For God's sake, He was in His thirties, unmarried, and hanging around with twelve guys. What would people in 1963 think of that? The one guy I met who I knew was queer because he had told the truth, asked if I was too, and when I said "No," he had backed off. This, of course, was something that wasn't done by Phil, a kid who everyone liked and thought of as normal, even though he would not listen to Jane when she said, "No." So, I thought, who's the sinner here?

If I was going to find out where I belonged, I felt the rules of my religion all by themselves weren't going to tell me.

The rules of the streets were fun, but the streets of Milford were different from the streets of South Phoenix, and the streets of Hopedale were kind of a joke. In Hopedale, Mike was idolized for punching people in the face, and the smartest kid in the school was laughed at because the doctor told her to wear the wrong kind of shoes.

My mother's rules made the most sense when she would open up and tell us her actual rules, but she focused instead on helping us fit in wherever we were, which would have been fine if we had only stopped moving long enough to fit in somewhere.

It was obvious to me, at seventeen, that the only rules that would work for me would be the rules that were mine alone. I was determined to find those rules.

Then the world changed. I had decided to skip school one day because Diane's new kid needed a babysitter.

I couldn't let her down. As I pulled into the driveway at her house, the announcer on the radio broke into the middle of the song, "I'm Leaving It Up To You" by Dale and Grace. "We interrupt this program with an important announcement." *What the hell?* I thought. *What happened?* I sat in the driveway and listened, dumbfounded. John Kennedy had been shot. Assassinated. Dead. He had been the first Catholic to be elected President, and it was like losing a father. It left a hole in every Catholic heart. From then on, the country seemed to become more purposeful, more serious. So did I.

Chapter Nine
NEAR DEATH EXPERIENCE

*I*N MY SENIOR YEAR, I came to the realization that I wanted to go to college. After the debacle with Cecelia, I had managed some dates with girls, all of whom I felt were pretty much out of my league. Some I had to take to a movie or a dance, but some would opt for driving out to the woods to help me finish a six-pack. I didn't worry too much about dating, though. I had other things to worry about.

My grades sucked, and my only friendly teachers were Mr. D, Mr. Katz, and Mrs. Marion. They all agreed I should further my education. Pat had graduated from college and planned on marrying a classmate. She said she would help with the tuition. Now I just had to find a cheap college who would take me if I got better grades in my final year.

Senior year began as I had wanted it to. My good luck

in the dating department kept me from getting in as many brushes with drinking and the law, and my life began to calm down.

I had a job at a supermarket, and I had begun to turn over my new leaf by studying and even got myself put onto a committee to help find fundraising ideas for the class.

Then something happened.

I was driving Danny, a friend who lived near me, home from school in early spring when he turned to me and said, "I think that shit that happened to your brother Dennis sucked."

"What happened?" I asked, only half interested.

"He got thrown off the bus by that new driver. It happened down by the Ford dealership. He had to walk a couple miles."

"For what?"

"He said Dennis swore at him, but everyone says it wasn't Dennis."

"So he walked home. That's no big deal."

"No, he *threw* him off the bus. He told him to get off, and then when he got up and went to the door, the driver shoved him off the last step into the dirt. He closed the doors and drove off."

"You're right, that does suck. I'll talk to Dennis about it,' I said.

I didn't get a chance to talk to my younger brother that afternoon, but when I drove downtown to sit on the one-way street with my friends, I noticed a school bus carrying the baseball team back to the gymnasium from an away game. Screwhead walked over to my window and leaned down. "Hey, the guy driving that bus is the guy who shoved your little brother in the street today."

I got out of the car, not having any idea what I might do, but as I walked toward the bus and saw the driver standing outside the door, I got more and more angry. Dennis was a good kid. There was no way this guy was going to get away with hurting him.

"Hey, you," I said as I walked down the length of the school bus, from the back to the front door where the driver stood, and I confronted him. My entire being of five foot nine, a hundred and thirty-five pounds, was astonished that the guy looked scared as he smoked his cigarette. When he lifted it toward his mouth, I slapped it out of his hand.

"You like shoving little kids into the road?" I asked.

His head moved backward as if to avoid me. "He deserved it."

I grabbed his shirt with both hands and pushed him up against the bus.

"No, he didn't. He wasn't the one who swore at you. You got the wrong kid."

I banged his head against the bus. "You shoved him into the dirt."

"If he was the wrong kid, I'm sorry," the driver said.

"You're sorry, and if he gets on your bus again, you won't give him any shit, will you?"

"He can get on the bus," he said. I let go, and he climbed back into the safety of the bus.

I thought I had handled it well and taken care of the matter.

The next day, Friday, I'd been suspended from school for a week. I guess it wasn't over.

I expected my grades would take a severe hit.

The school told me I wouldn't be allowed back into school until my parents met with Mr. York, the Superintendent of Schools.

They set up a meeting at his office at night. My father said he would meet me there.

Around 8:30, I walked from the pool room over to the school and sat on the front steps. My father arrived a few minutes later.

I first noticed his collar stood up in the back. He'd never worn it like that before. His hands were shoved deep in his pockets as he walked up to me, his black hair perfect. As he got close to me, he winked and smiled.

"We have to go meet with this asshole who pushed Dennis into the dirt?"

"I guess." I said, and it occurred to me that although he wasn't drunk, he had been drinking.

"Well, let's go see him."

I followed him up the steps of the school.

We walked into a darkened school building. My father stopped, and I pointed to the only room that had a light shining out from under the door.

As we walked inside, I noticed Mr. York sitting complacently behind his desk, an even bigger desk than Mr. Kent's. I smiled, thinking that these people must have felt that their importance in the world might actually be determined by the size of their desks.

"Where is this bus driver?" my father asked while we were still standing just inside the office door.

"The bus driver won't be coming," York said with finality.

"Okay Jocko, then you don't have to be here either."

"Oh, but he does," York said.

"Why?" Dad asked.

"Because I have to determine what is going to be done with him."

Dad backed up a few steps and opened the door.

"You're going to determine what I am going to do with my son?" he asked. He motioned to me. "Skeedaddle," he said. I did, but I took a quick glance at York as I left the two men inside the room, and I realized it was the only place in the otherwise empty building that had a light on. York's eyes were wide, his mouth hung open, and his hand twitched. He had just realized that he was no longer in charge.

"Go on, get out," Dad said. "The big boys have to talk."

I sat on the steps for about a half hour. Dad came out. As he sat down beside me on the steps, he said, "You go back to school Monday. The driver got fired."

I began to get up, but he reached over and pulled me back onto my step by the shoulder.

After a few quiet minutes, he said, "Do you remember those Mexican families we worked with in the cotton fields?"

"Right," I said. "One of them was named 'Hey-soos.'"

He lit a cigarette, and I got a kick out of the fact that he was sitting on the steps of the school smoking. He continued, "They came by truck every day into a place where most people didn't like them. They put their heads down, ignored the crap, and they worked. They made enough money to feed their families at home. They put up with the bullshit of those redneck field bosses because their goal was to take care of themselves and their families. They knew a lot of the bosses were jackasses, but they only stood up to them when it mattered, like when the guy decided not to pay you, and that big black guy stood behind you and made him pay. Remember that?"

I nodded.

"You know," he said, "when the Irish came over here, they called us 'niggers turned inside out.'"

I turned to him. He had never used that word in front of me before, and he never did again, but I guess he felt what he was going to say in that moment was important enough to get my attention.

"When your grandfather got here, he was a crazy teenage farmer, but he worked every kind of job you could imagine. He got beat senseless by a New York cop and then joined a gang for protection. Then, a lot of years later, when I got out of high school, I was the first in my family to graduate. He told me what I'm telling you now. It is your lot in life to go further than your father did. Each son has to raise the family a little higher on the food chain."

"I don't understand that," I said.

"It means you'll have to put up with a little of the same crap Buster has to put up with. Some people think there are different rules for them and for you. They think they can get away with treating you like you're less than them. Just like Buster had to put up with Jim Crow."

I thought about my treatment by the principal, Mr. Kent. "You're an Irish punk from Milford, so that's two strikes," he had told me, even though I had always been proud to be Irish and from Milford.

"Have you seen that?" Dad asked.

"Yup, I've seen it," I answered.

"You can do one of three things when you see it," he said. "You can either let it go, or you can fight, or, if they get too big for you, you can call me. If you're going to take care of it yourself, be ready to deal with the consequences. I just explained that to Mr. York."

He turned to me and asked, "Are you listening to me?"

"Yes," I said. "I'm listening."

"It's important. Always weigh the consequences of what you are going to do. Sometimes it's worth the punishment. Sometimes it's not. It was worse for me than it is for you, and it was even worse for your grandfather, and Buster, a better man than most of us, has to put up with the worst of it." He flipped his cigarette away, bent down in front of my face, and turned toward me. "It will get better for your kids too, but for you, you'll still feel the weight of the people who press down on you to make themselves feel a bit lighter about themselves. Sometimes you gotta let it go."

"I don't know how to let it go," I said.

"Think of the bullshit Buster has to go through. You remember Buster, don't you?"

"I do."

"Think of how many times he has to bite his tongue just to survive, because he's a Negro. Sometimes you have to bite yours too, because you're Irish. Don't get me wrong. The shit is not as bad for us as it is for him, but it comes from the same pile o' dung."

"When do I fight?"

"You fight when it will make a difference. If it won't make a difference, bite your damned tongue and duck your feckin' head."

We both laughed a little.

We stood up from the stone steps. "So, I should have left the bus driver alone?"

"Hell no. You did the right thing. You shoulda slapped him silly. York knows that now. Let's go home."

I returned on Monday, determined to work harder. My grades got better, and I took the SATs, even though I had a hangover. I was dating a girl named Peggy at the time. She made sure I got to the test. Like I said, the girls I dated were out of my league. I did as well on the test as most of the kids who were going to top schools, and it seemed possible I might make it into a college after all.

I applied to a college called Worcester Junior. Everyone called it Whoopie J, but it was a college, and I expected I would be going. I wouldn't be the first in my family to go to college. My sister Patty had already done that, but I was taking a step above what my father had done, and he had told me that was my goal in life, to do better than my father so my kids could do better than me.

Coming from the Kraft Dinners and third-hand clothes of my early life, I figured it shouldn't be all that hard to climb a step or two.

My grades continued to go up, and the teachers who were friendly to me were happy with my efforts. They all liked to take credit for my "turnaround."

A few weeks later, in a study hall, I went to the teacher's desk and asked for a pass to go to the boys' room.

She handed me a pass. Then she handed me a folded piece of paper and said with a smile, "Could you first take this to the office?"

"Sure," I said.

Outside the room, I opened the folded piece of paper. It read, "What are we going to do about Dennis Hourihan? I want him suspended."

I figured Dennis would have to face his own consequences for his own actions, but I wasn't going to help get him his punishment. I wouldn't want him to think I approved of this. I walked back into the room. It mattered what my little brother thought of me, so I decided to fight. I went back inside the room. I walked directly and purposefully to her desk, stood, and stared at her until she raised her head from the papers she was correcting. She adjusted her glasses and said, "What?"

"What makes you think I'm your delivery boy?" I asked.

She eyed the crumpled paper on her desk and then turned to me. "Did you read that?" she asked.

"Of course I read it. Any kid in this school would have read it, and you know it. You think it's funny to make me bring the note to the office that gets my brother suspended. You jerk. Deliver it yourself." I turned from her desk and went to the boys' room. There was a smattering of applause as I left.

I returned to Mr. Kent waiting for me.

"Okay, punk. You are suspended for two weeks."

"There's only one week left of school, and it's all finals," I said.

"That's the beauty of it," Kent said. "You don't get to take your finals, and you don't get to graduate. Get out!"

All the things I could say or do passed in front of my eyes, but, luckily, I ignored them, turned, and started out of the school, but as I passed the office the school secretary, Mrs. Dec, called to me through the open office door.

"John, come here," she said.

I turned on my heel, went back to the office, and stood in the doorway.

"There's a phone call for you," she said.

"What?" This, of course, was unheard of. Students didn't get phone calls at school.

I waited for the joke.

"Really," she said and reached over the desk to hand the phone toward me.

I stepped into the office, walked behind the chest-high island that usually kept students at bay, and I took the phone from her hand.

"Hello," I said cautiously.

"This Jack Hourihan's kid?" The voice was harsh, and even more so when being heard inside a school where people very rarely said what they were thinking.

"Right," I said.

"You better get your ass down here to the shop. He's real sick or drunk or something. I don't know which."

I dropped the phone and nearly ran from the building.

I drove my parents '62 Dynamic 88, Oldsmobile. And every one of the eight cylinders worked its best as I flew from Hopedale the six or so miles to Depot Street in Milford and Bickford Shoe. I slammed on the brakes in the middle of the dirt parking lot and flung myself out the door before the car had stopped sliding. I ran up the rickety, outside, wooden stairs to the second-floor office, knocked, pushed the heavy door open, and rushed inside.

My father, Scrapper Jack Hourihan, this cast-iron Irishman, this superman of my life, sat on a backless wooden chair and slumping forward onto the dust-covered desk. His right hand clutched his left arm. His shiny face projected a whitish green hue, and his sweat soaked right through his shirt. My stomach churned to see the man who had been the strength of my life being crushed beneath the weight of his own life.

I looked at the floor boss, who stood across the room against the wall, doing nothing. I picked up the black phone on the desk.

"Hey, what the fuck are you doing, kid?"

"I'm calling an ambulance," I said, and dialed zero.

"We ain't paying for any fucking ambulance," the boss

said. He rushed across the room and reached to take the phone out of my hand.

It felt as if my father's strength had been lost to him but had been transferred to me as I slapped the man's hand away and pushed him with one hand in the center of his chest backwards until he stumbled back against the wall where he had been in the first place. As I walked away from him, the woman operator said, "Can I help you?"

"Yes, I need an ambulance at Bickford Shoe on Depot Street in Milford."

The boss took a step forward, but I pointed at him and stared my father's intimidation stare into his eyes. He stopped.

"What's the problem?" the operator asked.

"A man is having a heart attack," I said.

"He's not having a heart attack," the boss said. "He's drunk."

I covered the mouthpiece of the phone. "Right, well, he's drunk a lot. I know what that's like. This ain't it. This is a heart attack. The ambulance is on its way. You got any whiskey around here?"

He reached up on a shelf and handed me the bottle.

"Here dad, have a swig of this. It will help thin your blood."

His eyes pleaded with me like I must have with him from time to time when I was a kid. Somehow I saw the eyes of my dog Seabee when he got hit by a car and lay dying on the side of the road. A cop friend of my father's had arrived and shot him. The cop had said he'd had to "put him out of his misery." I hit the cop in the head, right between the eyes, with a rock. I said it was because "you pissed me off by shooting my dog."

The five minutes it took for the big white and red panel-truck ambulance to arrive screaming its siren down the street seemed like a lifetime.

I watched my father sinking onto the desk. I had always been able to handle myself in nearly any situation, even if the ultimate outcome was to "run like hell," but there were times when I just couldn't, and he was always there to say, "skeedaddle," and close the door behind me while he handled the problem. Now, it seemed, my turn had come.

I thought of John Kennedy, and then of my own father. What would I do if he died? I thought. I heard the wail of the siren entering the parking lot. I saw the bustle of motion while they carried the stretcher up the stairs and into the office. The paramedics carried him out on the stretcher and vacantly assured me my father would be okay, even though they had no idea if he would or not.

I turned to his boss, ready to deal with the man.

"We ain't paying for that," he said.

"Fuck you," I answered. "You'll pay for it, or I'll burn this fucking place to the ground." I only stared at him long enough so he wouldn't see the fear behind the threat. Then I turned and walked out the door. Eventually, the shop owner paid for the ambulance.

My father was safely on his way to the hospital, and I was back to normal; sitting in the front seat of a black Oldsmobile, behind the wheel, and shaking uncontrollably.

I followed them to the hospital, where I used a pay phone to call my mother and let her know what had happened. Scrapper Jack survived, but his brush with death had sobered him, sort of, and only for a short time. Unlike Kennedy, he hadn't died. However, he retired from work that day. I guess relying on the strength of fathers past this point probably wasn't the best idea in the world.

That night, I bought a quart of Jack Daniels and drove out to the top of Bare Hill overlooking Milford. I sat on the hood of the car and drank, watching the moon rise above the town. The loss of our house, when I was a kid, returned to me in my half-drunken state. It occurred to me that the guy at the bank who had overseen taking our house had never been punished for that. I capped the quart and climbed back into the car. I drove back into town and straight to the road where I knew the bank guy lived. I parked a few houses down from his.

I walked to the front door and checked my watch, the hands reading nearly midnight. I had no idea what I intended to do, just that somehow I would make him pay, I guess.

I rang the doorbell and waited. It took a while, but then the door opened a crack.

"Can I help you?" she asked.

The wife of the bank guy stood in front of me, a surprisingly young and pretty redhead.

"Is Garrett here?" I asked.

"No, Garrett doesn't live here anymore," she answered, but she opened the door farther.

She wore a lightweight, white summer robe, pulled tight and tied around the waist.

"Oh," I said. "My car broke down, and I realized he lived here, so I thought I would be able to use your phone to call someone to pick me up."

"Oh," she said, and she stepped back a half step, thought for only a few seconds and then said, "Well, sure. Come on in." She opened the door all the way and gestured me inside. I noticed the robe only covered part of her legs and ended somewhere above her knees.

My hands and stomach shook in fright. What I decided now to do was probably not very nice, but I wanted to do what he had done to my family, take something away from him that had meant life and death to him, like our home had to us.

We walked into the kitchen, and she turned on the light over the table. "The phone is right here on the wall," she said.

"Thank you." I picked up the phone and began dialing. After three or four numbers, I switched hands with the phone, and in the switch, I laid my finger on the return, hanging up the phone for just a second. After I dialed the rest of the numbers, the phone pressed tightly against my head still hummed its dial tone.

"Hi, Mike, could you pick me up? My car broke down." I waited for the length of what might have been his answer, then said, "Great, okay, half an hour." I hung up.

When I turned back, she sat at the kitchen table, legs

crossed and eyes focused on me..

"Sit down," she said. "You can wait in here."

I sat across the table from red hair and green eyes. Even though she was probably in her mid-thirties, she looked younger.

"How old are you?" she asked.

"Nineteen," I lied. She smiled. I think she knew I was lying.

"So," I asked. "How come Garrett doesn't live here? Are you divorced?"

"No. Not divorced. We're just separated for a while. We're… trying to work some things out."

She reached up and scratched her shoulder beneath her robe, leaving it more open than it had been before. I could now see her cleavage. I looked back to her face. She had seen where my eyes had been.

I decided then that, since he had our home, I would have his wife.

"So," she said. "Someone is picking you up?"

"A friend."

"Where does your friend live?"

"In Hopedale."

"So he'll be a little while?" she asked.

"I suppose so."

"Would you like a drink?"

"Sure," I said.

She got up and went into the next room, and in a few minutes, I heard her call me.

"Come on in here. It's more comfortable."

I walked into the next room and realized two drinks had been poured and put on the coffee table. She sat on the couch, and her robe had inched up a few inches. As I reached the couch and sat down, she leaned forward and pushed my drink toward me. As she did, her robe opened up more, and I could see that she was slowly exposing herself. It seemed to me to be on purpose. My payback to the man who had taken our home was going to be easier than I had intended. It seemed his wife intended a little payback herself.

But then something went wrong.

I must have sobered up, and a voice that had always echoed in my head chose that moment to tell me that what I was doing was wrong, even if she seemed to want the same thing. It occurred to me that there was misery in this home, and I was just adding to it. I couldn't do that. I tossed down the drink, put the empty glass on the coffee table, and said, "I think I just saw headlights. I think I'll wait in the car. But thank you for the drink and the phone call."

"I don't think he's here yet," she said, walking with me to the door.

"Bye, thanks," I said and left, almost falling down the front steps.

I went back to the car and left, thinking, *Maybe I am some kind of half-assed soldier of Christ after all. I couldn't go through with what I had planned, because it was wrong, even if it would have been easy and most likely a lot of fun.*

Chapter Ten
TO GROW UP, YOU FIRST HAVE TO STAY ALIVE

I WASN'T DONE DRINKING, and I decided that weekend, with my father still in the hospital readying for angioplasty, that I would finish the bottle of Jack I had started. I began my Saturday morning getting dressed and realizing I really needed to buy some new underwear.

That afternoon, I sat in the parking lot of the Ten Pin, facing the road and watching the cars when suddenly in the right-hand passenger side window a face popped up that I would have recognized if it wasn't all hamburgered up. The red and swollen face of my friend Pete peered in the side window, and he motioned for me to roll it down.

"What the hell happened to you?"

"We got beat up pretty good down in Franklin."

"Yeah, pretty good," I said as I leaned over and unlocked the door so he could get in.

He and a friend we called Mumbles had gone down to Franklin to visit a girl they had met at a Friday night dance at Lakeview Park, and somehow he got pummeled.

His face was pulp, his nose swatted over to the side and red. His eyes were already turning black, and the blood vessels in his right eye were all busted. Mumbles only got his ribs kicked a bit, maybe cracked.

Everyone had vowed revenge. Late that afternoon, we all piled into cars and drove to Renda's Market in The Plains to see who would go with us, since Pete had family who were close to the Milford kids.

Big Teddy Bear and his cousin Manny decided Pete and Mumbles had been wronged, and they said they would go with us. But as we crossed the line into Franklin, we were confronted by Gilley.

Gilley was big, and he wasn't a kid. Reputation said he had finished a stint in both the Army and the Massachusetts Correctional Institution Cedar Junction, and he stood in the middle of Route 140 waiting for the caravan full of the child warriors of retribution.

I would be willing to bet that the fifty or so Franklinites lining the shoulders of the road all hated Gilley as much as we did. With a mean and nasty temper, I'm sure most of those on his side had been beaten by him at one time or another. He stood in the middle of the highway with an ax handle. On one end was an ax, on the other a five-pound sledge, and he swung it around his blond head like a Ninja baton twirler.

The men and boys on the sides of the road were armed

with every manner of farm implement, switch blade, club, and tire iron.

Our caravan turned around right there in the road, drove back a mile or so and stopped to huddle.

"We got enough guys," Teddy shouted, "but I think we are seriously out tooled."

Manny suggested our options.

"We can fight them now, or we can get more guys and more tools and come back later."

Until that day, I had, like any teenager, been willing to say or do any stupid thing in the world just to be accepted. Because of recent events, however, for me, that blind need for acceptance by idiots had begun to wane. On that day, I decided on the other option that Manny hadn't mentioned.

I clandestinely motioned my friends back into the car. They got in, not because I was in charge, but because I was their ride.

Inside the Olds, I turned sideways in my seat so I could see all four and said, "I'm not sure what we're doing here. Mumbles and Pete didn't even come. I don't know who asked us to come here and get killed, or what good it will do if we win. I have a better idea what we can do with the day."

I drove to K-Mart to buy some underwear.

"No one goes looking for a fight at K-Mart," I explained as I pulled into the parking lot.

That night I was glad I grew up in time to not die in the road that day. No one else went back either.

On Monday, the first day of my newest suspension, I sat

at the kitchen table with Mum having a late breakfast when the phone rang. I placed my spoon at the edge of my bowl of Froot Loops and stood up to answer the green wall phone.

"Hello, John?"

I recognized the voice. I had heard it before, but not on the phone.

"Yes."

"This is Mr. Dooley."

I had never gotten a call from the school before, especially not from the vice-principal.

"Oh, okay, what do you want?"

"Well, a few things here at school have changed."

The words of Principal Kent rang back into my head: "That's the beauty. You won't take your exams. You won't graduate," he had said with a smile.

"You're going to graduate," Mr. Dooley said.

"I am?"

"Well, if you take and pass all your exams."

"When?"

"In three weeks."

"But graduation is in one week."

"You'll graduate with your class, but the diploma will be blank. It will just have your name on a sheet of paper. After you pass your exams, you will get the real one."

I smiled across the table to my mother, who sat waiting patiently, sipping her tea.

"Why do I think you had something to do with this, Mr. Dooley?" I asked.

"Well, I might have helped it along, but you were passing

all your classes, so you had a hand in it too."

"Thanks, Mr. D."

"You're welcome. Oh, John, you had better study. They aren't going to give you the same exams your class is getting."

"Well, I figure they wouldn't… They would be afraid I'd cheat, right?"

"No, I mean, the exams are very difficult. Much more difficult than, well… You had better study hard."

"Okay. When is my first exam?"

"The Monday after graduation."

"It figures. They wouldn't want to give me too much time to study, would they?"

"John, don't be like that. Some people stood up for you, and some of your teachers too. You could have been expelled and lost any chance at graduation if they hadn't."

"I know. I'm sorry. Thanks again. I'll be ready."

"Oh, and your committee has asked if you can be at their meeting for the class fundraiser."

I twirled the phone cord around my hand. "Is that okay?" I asked.

"I guess it can't hurt. It's tomorrow at 10:45 in the cafeteria."

I hung up the phone and looked across the kitchen table at my mother.

"I'm going to graduate," I said.

She smiled. "Good," she said and finished her tea.

I drove into the student parking lot and, hoping I

wouldn't see Kent, I walked in the side door that entered the school through a door adjacent to the cafeteria. The others were already there. They were class officers. I was not, and I wondered how I'd ever been named to the committee in the first place. The four had been waiting for me to arrive. Then Mrs. Marion walked in, and I realized she was the reason I was here. She told me later she felt it would be good on my college application. I guess she had figured that out before I got myself suspended.

"Let's get started," she said. "What have we come up with?"

Steve, the president of our class, had an idea.

"I thought we could have a basketball tournament," he said.

"How will that make money?" she asked.

"We could have each class put together a basketball team and put up an entry fee. The winner would get a plaque in the trophy case, and our class would get the entry fees."

"What do you think?" she said to the rest of us.

A few of the officers nodded.

There were other ideas; raffles, a lottery, a bake sale.

"I think the basketball tournament is a great idea," I said. "Let's vote on it."

The rapid agreement took the others by surprise, and we voted unanimously to have a basketball tournament. Because of my support, Steve was ready to side with me on the next thing I said.

"We need to call it something," I added.

Everyone turned to Mrs. Marion. She shrugged.

"How about something innocuous," I said. "Like the senior high invitational tournament?"

There were nods of agreement, a vote, and it was slam dunk. We set the fee at $200, and we disbanded.

A few days before graduation, and a few weeks before school got out for the underclassmen, the tournament took place. Outside the gymnasium, flapping in the breeze, the four-foot-deep banner that spanned the entire top of the building read, Senior High Invitational Tournament.

Only the enlarged and capitalized letters stood out, S-H-I-T in bright Raider blue.

I couldn't be blamed. It had been voted on and supported by the committee and the teacher-supervisor. It was deemed an innocent mistake.

Next came the graduation.

We got to set up our own chairs on the lawn of the Community House the day before we were to graduate.

Of course, when we set up the public address system, we all got to take turns singing "Louie Louie" to the cars that were driving by. The clandestine and filthy words, known only to teenagers, echoed off the drug store, the police station, the Unitarian church, and General Draper's high school.

The next day, I showed up at the cafeteria where the caps and gowns were being handed out.

I stood just inside the door and watched my classmates foraging for their individual gowns, Raider blue for the boys and deceptively innocent white for the girls. They beamed as they pulled them on over their heads and tried on their caps.

Four years ago, I had stepped off the bus outside this school and assessed the gauntlet of students waiting to watch the new kid walk through. They all knew each other then, and they didn't know me.

They knew me now.

Mr. Katz walked over to me and handed me my gown.

"You did it, Hourihan," he said. "Good job."

"I have a feeling I had some help," I answered, and we both laughed.

"Don't forget to thank Mrs. Marion," he said.

Outside on the street, in the June warmth of the blanket of a protective small town, in the comfortable shadow of the Universalist church, and with General Draper High School urging us gently from behind, we lined up two by two. We were nervous and anxious to get this over with so we could get to our graduation parties. We each knew whose parents would have an open bar and which would serve minors. We were facing down Dutcher Street. I had been told it was named after a guy whose invention had been usurped by the shop that we had been trained to work at if we didn't go to college. A mansion rose on the right side of the street, the Universalist Church on the left. The branches of the horse chestnut trees lining the street just after the church reached parentally across to cover the road high above the street. Then, across from the gym and after the church, sat the Community House, a large stately brick building that was the pride of the town and the site of our graduation.

We marched to a wobbly version of Pomp and Circumstance down the street. Each student, except for me and a very few others, probably remembered his or her kindergarten first day together with nearly everyone else here, each remembering the entry into high school together.

The College Course third of the class wondered about what higher education would feel like in some far away town or city, and how far the two-hundred-dollar scholarships they were anticipating would take them. The Business Course kids were wondering just where they would be getting a job and what they were going to do with the Spanish language they had learned, since no one in a hundred-mile radius spoke Spanish except this group. The General Course students could see, a block down the street, the huge brick factory where their life waited for them. We passed the parents, the teachers, and the town officials who had come to give speeches and garner favor from the Draper bosses. Cars passing on Hopedale Street slowed down and blared their horns.

We filed down the cement walkway to our seats that we had set up the day before on the wide cement stairway overlooking the rows of parents seated on the lawn.

The day couldn't be more perfect. The grass in front of us was deep green and mowed meticulously, and the sky was Hopedale Raider blue. I searched for God in the sunlight over the pinnacle of the Community House but didn't see Him. Then I remembered this town was based on secular humanism, where those in charge actually believed you could be a good human being without believing in something larger than us.

I sat through the speeches and the five-and ten-dollar "scholarships." We all sat sweating in our woolen caps and gowns, smelling of moth balls and body odor, while an endless string of town politicians and educators mumbled tips for achieving the American Dream to the blind applause of parents, some of whom had not been allowed to work in this town, some who were underpaid and under-appreciated in the shop, some who had not been allowed to swim in the town pond, or even pass the doors into this Community House. Some of the parents had expected this outcome from the time their perfect little Unitarians entered kindergarten; others were pleasantly surprised at the outcome; still others were perfectly stupefied and would say a rosary of thanks tonight.

Then the valedictorian took the microphone. She was the girl with the orthopedic white bucks. As she gave her speech, I could see the blood drain from the faces of the adults who knew exactly what Hopedale was. It was 1964, and she spoke of equal rights for women in the face of home economics classes that were mandatory for all girls in General Draper High School. She spoke of outside opportunity for all those in the graduating class who wanted more from Hopedale than myriad months of practicing shorthand, and I wondered what brave teacher had approved that speech. When she finished, the silence lasted for five or six interminable seconds. Then one of our classmates, Jim, stood up and purposefully began to applaud slowly. The rest joined in, some of us out of agreement with Jim, but most out of embarrassment.

And then the big scholarships of hundreds of dollars were announced. Next came the call of the roll.

Each graduate in his or her turn was called to the podium by Kent to be handed a blue plastic folder holding a high school diploma. Each graduate in turn dutifully said the words we had been told were appropriate, "Thank you, Mr. Kent," and returned to a seat.

When they called my name, I looked at him and knew he was about to have a wonderful time handing me a blue plastic diploma-covering filled with a piece of paper with my name on it, but nothing else. After all, I was an Irish punk from Milford, and he wasn't.

The freedom I felt in the woods of Purchase Street returned, as did the days of throwing a rock at the Irish Need Not Apply sign in our barn. The desert barrio of South Phoenix pumped my blood pneumatically into my brain, and I weighed the advice of my father on the night we sat on the steps of the school building. I thought of the consequences of my actions and decided what I was about to do was worth any punishment they could come up with.

He reached out his sweaty little hand for me to shake and smiled into my eyes. I felt as if I was seeking goodness in the eyes of a demon. "Congratulations, Hourihan," he said, and he almost laughed out loud.

"Fuck you, Mr. Kent," I answered calmly and with a

smile. I took the fake diploma and walked back to my seat. I sat down and watched him. His face remained frozen in that sarcastic smile. He hadn't even called the next name.

I wondered how many people realized I hadn't said, "Thank you, Mr. Kent." I mean, a microphone stood right next to him, and there had been a short murmur in the crowd when I walked back to my seat.

I drank myself silly that night, then I went home and for weeks I studied.

I passed everything. According to Mr. D, I had hardly gotten anything wrong.

A few days later, I went to the office and got my diploma. It sat unceremoniously inside a manila envelope in the mailbox outside the principal's office.

That same day, I received in the mail an acceptance letter from Worcester Junior, but first I had to take a trip up to the college to meet with the dean.

I sat in my family car in the back parking lot of the junior college in Worcester and watched students walking freely in and out of the back door. They were obviously older than the kids I had just graduated with. They seemed to have more purpose in their stride, more confidence.

Maybe now I could turn over that new leaf I had promised my mother, maybe now I could grow up some.

I followed them inside and sat in the hallway in the first of the row of chairs outside the dean's office while a few others had their interviews, then it was my turn.

I entered the office and sat down in front of his desk. "Mr. Hourihan," he said. "I've been waiting for this."

"Me too, sir," I said.

"Tell me, why do you want to go to college?"

"So my family can jump a rung on the food chain," I answered, remembering Dad's words. "My father told me it is my job to help my family move up past where he got." I returned the dean's stare and asked, "Why did you accept me?"

I don't think he was prepared for me to be asking him questions.

After a short silence, he said, "Fair enough. I wanted to see you because this is the first time a teacher has written an unsolicited letter of not-recommendation." He watched my confused face, smiled, and added, "Your French teacher has written to us." He stopped and asked, "You didn't ask her for a recommendation, did you?"

"No," I said, wondering what he meant.

He picked up a piece of paper from his desk, glanced at it, and said, "Well, she wrote one anyways, and she says we shouldn't allow you to attend our school. I guess, from this letter, that she believes you are the spawn of the devil?"

"But you accepted me already," I said, a bubble of panic rising in my chest.

"Don't worry. We didn't pay attention to her. We paid attention to the other teachers who wrote recommendations. They kind of like you."

I knew I shouldn't say anything, just leave well-enough alone, but I couldn't help myself. "As to the spawn of the devil thing, I think she had a problem with my father when they were in high school together," I said.

We both laughed.

"That seems to be a possibility," he said. "Well, anyways, you have been accepted on the strength of your SATs, and I guess I will find out in September which of your teachers is telling the truth."

I shook his hand and left the office. As I walked down the hall and out to my car, I thought, *I guess I'm going to college. Damn.*

But before Woopie J, during that summer before college, I learned in a hospital emergency room that it is the seemingly small decisions, not the large, that determine the rest of our lives.

Chapter Eleven
MRS. MARION'S PREMONITION COMES TRUE

ONE SWELTERING SUMMER SUNDAY afternoon, the green eyes of Jimmy Kay held a world of hurt as the nurse pushed his wheelchair down the hall near the emergency room, followed closely by a local cop.

I had dislocated my shoulder during a collision at home plate in an impromptu afternoon baseball game. At the hospital, I leaned against the coffee machine, waiting for someone to work on me and fix my shoulder. The wheelchair went by, with Jimmy's head bobbing like one of those plastic dashboard white-haired troll dolls.

"Hey," I said, stopping the cop. "What's going on with him?"

I pushed myself off the coffee machine and winced with the pain in my shoulder, but the cop stopped and put a hand on my chest when I tried to get close enough to talk

Baltimore Catechism: Mass of the Faithful

with my friend from a couple of summers ago.

"This is none of your business," the cop said, making it clear I needed to back off.

I was headed for college, and my shoulder injury was pretty painful, so I nearly let it go at that.

The nurse backed the wheelchair against the wall at the triage station and started thumbing through forms.

Jimmy and I had spent most of a summer driving around nights in my sister's red VW bug in partially altered states. We were a lot alike and had gotten to be pretty close friends. He introduced me to the music of Phil Ochs, and I talked him out of joining the Army.

"The Army is the worst thing that could ever happen to you," I explained over the lip of my chosen drug, a Giant Imperial Quart of Narragansett. Drinking a GIQ in a VW bug was difficult, since, when I tried to drink, the bottom of the bottle hit the windshield. Jimmy sprawled next to me, eating hash and dropping acid. I had only started hanging out with him because I wanted to get to know his sister, which I had never done, but then we got along, and I started picking him up at night because I liked his company.

He was one of those eternally funny people who could make you laugh until your face hurt, and, if I wasn't going to get to meet his sister, I at least needed someone to laugh with.

This was the first time I had seen him since that summer.

I leaned back against the vending machine and stared across the room of plastic chairs, empty except for some skinny, unshaven old guy who kept moaning and rocking back and forth in pain from what appeared to be a lifetime of wrong decisions.

Triage was across the waiting room on the other side of the chairs about thirty feet from me, and I could see Jimmy's clouded eyes clearly in the bright light of the small office. He looked as if he had the mange — his mouse brown hair seemingly having fallen out in clumps. His skin was the consistency of oatmeal. His eyes were, for the most part, closed and weepy. I recognized the clothes — the black jeans and red flannel shirt — just like the ones he had worn when we were hanging out together, drinking and chasing women.

He lifted his head for a second, and our eyes met.

I nodded, and he smiled.

Two of his top teeth were missing, and the rest had begun to rot near the gum line. I walked over to the door to the office and mouthed, "What happened?" Then I realized he wasn't smiling at me. He wasn't smiling at anyone. He was just smiling.

The cop suddenly appeared in the doorway and asked, "Are you a friend of his?"

I nodded.

"What's his name? We found him down on Central Street, sitting next to a dumpster."

"I guess someone threw him away," I said.

The cop nodded.

I stepped into the office and helped fill in the forms as much as I could, and we found his sister's phone number and called her.

Jimmy Kay just sat in his chair and stared at me.

Vacant.

"Hey Jimmy," I tried, sidling my chair across in front of him. He recognized his name and now focused on me.

"I know you," he said. Then he went stone blank.

I looked at the cop for an explanation.

"Smack, I think," he said.

Just as they were taking me to have my shoulder fixed, Jimmy's sister came in the front door. She smiled at me in thanks.

They offered me a shot of Demerol for my shoulder pain. I said no.

Shit like this happens for a reason, I thought.

We are supposed to pay attention.

The next Friday, I went to night confession at Sacred Heart Church in Hopedale bent on cleaning the slate and, once more, trying to start over. I had started over so many times in the past few years I thought I might have sounded like a '41 DeSoto trying to start on a sub-zero morning in New England in February. Start over, start over, start over, stall, start over.

Right, the chances weren't good, but as an elderly woman wearing a long gray cloth coat and a black hat left the confessional, I stepped in, knelt down, and inside the sacred box of anonymity, I blessed myself and said, "Bless me father for I confess to almighty God and to you father that I have sinned."

"Just a second Mr. Hourihan. I need to use the men's room."

I heard the priest get up, and his black gown rustled as he left the confessional. I opened the door, leaned out, and called after him, "Father?"

He turned back quickly. "What? I'm in a hurry."

"You are not supposed to know who I am in the confessional."

He laughed. "You think we don't know who is confessing?" He waved his hand in dismissal of my obviously stupid assumption and left.

I left too. This priest was not part of the religion I grew up with. I wondered if the priests and nuns I grew up with would wave their hands in derision at my innocence for thinking the hierarchy of my religion would actually go by their own rules. Had it all been a fairy tale told by an idiot? Had I been the idiot?

I walked from the church, into the dark and nearly empty parking lot. I left the lot and crossed under the railroad bridge, across the traffic on Route 16 and into the center of town. I sat on the steps of the building where I had fake graduated. In the distance, I could hear a car burning out. *Probably at the end of Dutcher Street*, I thought. There was no smell here in town. The flowers had been scrubbed clean by the powdered yellow pollution from the shop, and the trees had turned antiseptic. On this hot summer night, there should have been a natural aroma, but all I could smell was my cigarette and the smoke from the foundry.

My current life was seemingly based on a broken family who had once been held together by a strong love but was now just trying to hold on, and by a slippery religion whose multiple-choice rules contradicted each other and didn't even hold its nuns and priests to its own professed laws. I lit another cigarette and walked along the dark and quiet street that led to the town park. It seemed to me that everyone regularly broke the rules of civil law, that religious law was determined person to person, and that the school I currently attended favored the rich and Protestant in deciding which kids to educate best.

My family was rapidly losing faith in my ability to turn over a new leaf, and so was I. My religion had turned its back on me when it determined that my five-year-old self was possessed by demons because I had punched one of their favorites.

The police I'd been raised to respect in Milford because they were my father's friends had become the mortal enemy of all my own friends, and this school existed in order to determine who would succeed in life, who would succeed in business, and who would work in the inferno known as Draper's foundry. It was sort of like deciding who would go to heaven, purgatory, or hell. Once a person was shoved into one of these slots, it became a near impossibility to get out.

I had one thing left in front of me that might turn out to be where I would find out who I was, where I came from, and where I would be going.

Whoopie J, here I come. I figured I would give higher

learning a shot.

When I got home that night, my sister Pat told me she wanted me to come live with her just outside Worcester so I could study without interruption. Since she agreed to pay my tuition, I figured I had to say yes, so I moved to a rural town with even less of a center than Hopedale's.

Each day I took a half-hour city bus ride to school, and I wore a sport coat and dress pants. I sat in the front row of each class, and I studied.

Maybe I shouldn't have studied.

In my math class during my first year in college, I learned set theory, which I had also learned in my first half of freshman year of high school at St. Mary's. It was the same stuff, and I did well parroting back what I had learned years before.

In History of Western Civilization class, I learned that the world was settled by white people and that Francis Bacon was an idiot who believed we humans could understand everything if we just inspected it using the scientific method. I remember thinking, *So tell me Francis, what was the first thought?*

In biology class, I learned that we humans began as primordial ooze, and then we grew into human beings, which, supposedly, negated all the work of the good nuns of St Joseph who from my first day in first grade told us, "God made you, children." There had been nothing in the *Baltimore Catechism* about primordial ooze.

I was the only one in English lit who understood that

the turtle on the highway in Steinbeck's Grapes of Wrath had humorous eyes not because of some turtle joke, but because he was walking into the setting sun, which meant he was going West like everyone else in the book. Then we read Shakespeare's Julius Caesar.

And, of course I enrolled in French class. I learned that the hottest girls in the school took French. So I did too.

Then one June morning, just before the end of freshman year, I was sitting on the wall outside the building where I had just finished French class, which I always attended, and a commotion rose from the city street in front of me. A young man with long blond hair and a beard had stopped the traffic so those following him could vent their frustrations in the middle of the Main Street.

It was my first protest march. The students from Clark University, a top-tier school situated just up the street a mile or so, were chanting "Hell no, we won't go," and "Stop Goldwater" and "Get out of Vietnam." It was 1965, and they were enthusiastic and determined. They were ahead of the time.

I took stock again of my life. I was not living with my family. I was decidedly at odds with my religion. I was no longer allowed to play baseball. The school I had just graduated from didn't like that I had even been present in its halls. The town I lived in used to tell Irish people to stay out. The shining heroes of my youth were now telling me nightly to get my ass across the street and away from the stores where decent people walked, and Whoopie J, this bastion of higher learning, sucked.

While the children I attended college with lined up to watch the protest march and began shouting from the sidewalks, "Get a haircut," and "Take a bath," and "America, love it or leave it," I made a decision. On my next birthday, I would change my life. I had realized my situation wasn't someone else's fault. I had learned from Shakespeare that the fault was not in the stars but in myself that I was an underling. The time had come to do something about that.

I wasn't sure what, just yet.

Chapter Twelve
A MAN STANDS UP

*F*IRST, BEFORE I COULD finalize any decision that would drastically change my life, I needed to finish up my summer. *This could be the last summer I spend as a kid*, I thought.

We sat in the stands at Westboro Speedway, amidst the exhaust smoke, the smell of burning rubber and burning hot dogs, and the sound of growling jalopies making endless left turns. We had all come to watch Millen enter his father's car in the demolition derby. I began to think back to where I had first begun to grow up.

It happened during a middle-of-the winter Friday night poker game at my house when I was about eight years old.

One night we kids, all seven of us Hourihan children, had been ripped out of a deep sleep in the North Purchase woods by five drunken voices slurring in unison the words to "Sweet Genevieve" through the frigid night air outside and the melodic pleas of, "Open the door and let us in."

Most of my siblings pulled the coats we wrapped up with tighter to their chins, but I jumped to the floor and went out to greet the happy troupe of drunks.

My father and his friends had been tossed from Tibby's bar again and showed up hungry for spaghetti, beer, and cards, and they wanted my mother to unlock the front door. When he became like this, a happy drunk, everything was fun.

I got to watch the game from the warmth on the wooden floor next to the kerosene stove. His friends included Wicki Nixon, Case-a-Minute Davey, Little Paulie, my mother's uncle "Sea-Bee" Cyr, and Scrapper Jack himself.

Before the game started, Wicki took the cards, shuffled, scanned the table, and said what he always did. "Let's have a fair and square game, boys."

A couple dozen hands in, I see Little Paulie palm a card and slip it under his leg. Later, he pulls it out to fill a heart flush and takes a big pot, smiling.

I edge closer on the wooden floor but staying within the circle of heat.

He does it again later to fill three sevens, takes another pot.

Then when he tries it again, he fumbles the card and it flops onto the floor while everyone else is filling Melmac plates with spaghetti and getting another Knickerbocker, and he steps on it.

"Paulie, you hungry?" my father asked.

"No," he lies, and he stares at me eyeing his foot.

When he leans to pick it up — fourth card into a game of seven-card stud — he gets caught.

"What you got there, Paulie?" Scrapper Jack asks and leans over sideways to see the card in Paulie's hand.

"Hey," Paulie says. "The damn kid must have been playing with the cards, and we been dealing without the queen of hearts all along."

He tosses it on the table.

I was shocked that he lied — and him sitting right across from the shelf with the cream-colored plastic statue of our Blessed Mother with the screw-off base for the rosary.

Everyone smiled at me.

My father shook his head, and they were just about to go back to dealing, but I couldn't let it slide. I couldn't let him lie right in front of the Blessed Virgin, so I stood up in my underwear to the tallest four-foot-one inch I could muster and stared him down.

"You're a God Damn liar," I said.

He laughed. "Nice mouth," he said, but he was nervous. I could see it in his eyes.

"And you're cheating." I knew from the cowboy movies we watched that these were fighting words, and I wondered if that applied to little kids, too.

Now I was on the spot. Everyone turned to me in the musty yellow light.

Wicki, a tremendously religious man with Dagwood Bumstead hair, peered over his black-rimmed glasses at me for a long time. I snitched a peek at the statue.

I figured he was staring because I had taken the Lord's name in vain, but then he said, "I believe Johnny."

"He hid the seven last time," I said, "under his leg."

He'd a killed me if he could have, but Uncle Sea-Bee helped him out of the chair, and my father fished through Paulie's pockets for money as they bum's-rushed him to the door. They left him outside, in the cold, without his jacket, four miles from town, and broke.

When they get back, they give me his money, and for the first time they let me into the game.

"That was good," Davey said, wrenching his neck sideways at me as he shuffled. "A man stands up."

Then they proceeded to take all of Paulie's money from me, hand after hand, fair and square.

Truth is, I was scared to death but also shocked that he had lied, because to me it put a black mark in that white bottle of milk in the catechism book and would end him up in "Hell or Hopedale" as my father would have said.

At the time, Hopedale, to me, was just a dry town next to ours and as good as hell for shoe-shop pieceworkers like us. I only had the guts to stand up because I trusted that the Blessed Mother wouldn't let me take the rap for some cheating weasel like Little Paulie.

I felt Pete's punch in my arm, and the smell and rumble of Westboro Speedway came back to me.

"He's out there," he said.

He was right. Millen, driving his old man's station wagon, was in the middle of the line of junks getting ready for the night's demolition derby where they would all drive backwards around in circles, ramming into the other cars until only one remained in drivable condition. That one would be the winner. *A lot like my life,* I thought, *survival of the least demolished*, and I laughed to myself.

It never occurred to any of us that half of us now wouldn't have a ride home, since we came in the car that already had its right front fender wrapped up alongside the passenger-side window, and the driver's side door was missing.

The vehicle that had brought me here had been destroyed.

Millen had won fifty bucks, and we were now on our own.

All I could think of, while thumbing down Route Nine after the demolition derby took our ride, was, *What the hell is my family doing in Hopedale?*

I did a lot of thinking that summer and right into my sophomore year at Worcester Junior College. I went back to the halls of just-slightly-higher-learning in mid-September. I spent weekdays at my sister's house, and then on weekends I went home to Hopedale and began sinking into a deep, mostly hungover depression.

One day, my mother sat across from me at the kitchen table. I poked at my teabag inside the brown plastic cup with a spoon and waited for my aspirin to work when she slammed her hand down on the gray Formica tabletop to get my attention.

"What are you doing?" she nearly shouted. Sweet

Genevieve almost never nearly shouted, but this was one exception.

"What?" I asked, honestly confused.

"You were such a happy kid. No matter what happened, you got through it. Now you mope around being sad and doing nothing about it."

"I know, Mum. I'm working on it."

"Well, work faster," she said, dumped her tea into the sink, and left the room.

She was right.

I had been happy as a kid. I had been mostly happy throughout moving twelve times in eighteen years. I was happy through the cotton fields and knife fights of Phoenix, the poor days of little to eat, the exorcism in the first grade, taking a knife away from my father when he was drunk and threatening my mother. I had always had the constants of family, religion, baseball, and our Irish heritage.

I could see out the window the changing colors of the autumn leaves across the street from my house and thought back to when I was happy.

When I was born, WWII was just ending, the men had come home, and not everyone had a television, so husbands and wives got pretty familiar with each other, and as Mark Twain said, "Familiarity breeds contempt, and children," and my family had seven of them. Even though my father never went to war and remained embarrassed about it for the rest of his life, we too didn't have a TV.

Play time back then was organized, but organized by kids, not parents. After wolfing down a weekend morning bowl of Cream of Wheat, paying no attention to the skin color of the man on the box, we, each in the warmth of our own homes, began to suit up for a day in the woods. A Davy Crockett hat was essential. We all had one. Some had the plastic top that had the imprint of Fess Parker and Buddy Ebson, and some had the all-over fur.

There was always a Daisy Red Ryder BB gun (full magazine and a couple of cardboard reload tubes of BBs) and a black-handled hunting knife, slid into its leather sheath and threaded onto the gun belt. Next, we slid the leather hatchet cover onto the other side of the belt and snapped the hatchet into place. A black plastic-handled pocketknife with at least two blades and a can opener (only Peter Boy had an actual Swiss Army Knife. But his old man owned a diner, and we considered him to be rich.) Only one person I remember had a pistol that actually shot something. Jimmy D had a dart pistol powered by a CO_2 cartridge in the handle. It was by far the most dangerous utensil we had.

So there I appeared at the edge of the woods, coonskin cap, cloth coat, corduroy pants, PF Flyers, two knives, a hatchet, a Fanner 50 with the ricochet sound, and a BB gun. I headed for the Alamo, to defend it against Generalisimo Antonio Lopez de Santa Anna. This, of course, had been before I had learned he was a hero to some of the friends I made in the Arizona desert.

The rest showed up, seemingly just appearing out of the mist, in similar attire.

Some had pellet guns, some had bigger knives, and then

came Spike.

Spike carried a Bowie knife in its own leather sheath.

It went from up under his arm all the way to his knee. If he broke his leg, we could have used it as a splint.

We met — Spike, Peter Boy, Danny Mac, Jimmy D, and me — down behind the stinky-warmth of the chicken coops, across the brook, at the edge of the granite quarry.

We checked the safety clasps on the knives and hatchets, fired a BB off a tree trunk, and didn't cock the handle again before heading off into the woods, careful not to point the guns at each other.

For lunch, we would go to whichever house was closest, and somehow by magic, whoever's mother lived there would have tomato soup, bologna sandwiches or Kraft Dinner for us. We called them "M Rations." I guess they knew where we were, except Peter Boy's mother. That's how he got his name.

Somewhere around noon and again at sundown, the cry would echo across Goneau's field and pinball through the woods for miles to wherever we were. A loud and piercing "Peeeeeeterrrrrr boy, Time to come iiiiiiiiiiiiiin."

We packed food in our knapsacks, and we all had mess kits, and Peter Boy had a thermos for soup. We had morning meals in the woods, cut brush to make paths, built kips, fought Indians and Rebels and rustlers.

Then, every day, something miraculous would happen.

We would walk out of the woods — Me, Spike, Peter Boy, Jimmy D and Danny Mac — all in one piece. No one wounded, no one dead, and we would go home to listen to

"My Son Jeep" on the radio.

It was a happy time back then.

In the present, however, I finished my tea. It was mid-afternoon on a Sunday, and my sister Nancy was visiting. I had always been proud of my sister. She had been torn out of high school and made to go to work in the shoe shop, then in the Telechron, where assembly workers made clocks. She had been designated by my father to a life of piecework, and she had said, "Hell no!"

She quit work and got herself back into high school. By the time she had gotten married, she had her high school diploma.

My father never forgave her for that, but only when he drank.

I went out into the front yard and watched a twin engine plane take off into the October sky and thought how fantastic it would be to be able to fly off to anywhere you wanted, not being restricted by roads or highways or curfews. Not having to even come home every night. I sat on the rail fence in front of my house and smoked a cigarette. A quick glimpse at Cecelia's house made me smile. She and Richard were still a couple.

I flipped the cigarette into the road and went back into the house.

Mum returned and hovered over a new cup of tea. We sat at either end of the chrome-wrapped plastic table. To our right, the window showed the driveway and part of the front yard.

"You're right," I said. "I was a lot happier back then."

"Well, it's about time you figure out what made you happy, and do that," she said. "I'm getting a little fed up with your bullshit."

She never swore. I turned and smiled and noticed she wasn't smiling at all. She was, in fact, fed up with my bullshit. I guess I was too.

"You made it through having no teeth when you went to the first grade," she said.

That was true enough. I had fallen down the stairs and cracked all my teeth, and the dentist told my parents to "give him all the candy he wants and let them rot out." It was the cheapest way to go, but I showed up for first grade with my mouth full of black fangs.

"You made it through being introduced to all of your friends while you had penciled on eyebrows."

That had been true, too. I had been told by my sister that the implement I had just found in the bathroom on Purchase Street was "for pulling out your eyebrows," so I did.

"And you were happy. For God's sake, you made it through being exorcised by people you loved, and you came out smiling. What has happened to you? You even made it through the move to this horrible town, and you smiled. You got through this ridiculous school suspension, and you smiled. You have to get that back, that ability to smile thorough it all."

"I'm trying."

"Don't give me that crap. You've done it before. Do it again. What you are doing has to stop! Now!"

I turned back to the window. A taxi had pulled up to the end of the driveway. My father got out, reached in through the passenger window and paid the driver, and then he spun around and tried to walk into the driveway, but didn't make it. He tripped over nothing and fell onto the lawn. He pushed himself to a sitting position, surveyed the path to his side door, got up, fell again, got up and began aiming at the side door.

"Dad's home," I said.

A few seconds later, he stepped inside the door.

"What are you doing here?" he said when he saw me. "Don't you live in Rutland?"

"Oh, goody," I said. "It's going to be one of those days. Starting early, aren't you?"

"Shut up," he said, and moved into the other room, where he saw Nancy sitting on the steps that went from the living room to the bedrooms.

"And you. Too good to help us pay for this house. What is it with you girls? Couldn't you keep your legs closed? Did you all have to get married?"

"I didn't *have* to get married," she said.

My sisters loved my father even more than I did. When sober, he was a wonderful man and father, so it made it difficult to fight back when he was drunk.

This afternoon he focused on Nancy, and he lit into her with all the foul-worded gusto stored up during five hours of drinking twenty-five cent draughts. He wasn't expecting what happened next.

"Hey!" I shouted.

He spun and moved toward me from the other room. I stood in the doorway between the kitchen and the dining room.

"What?" he shouted back.

"Don't bring that barroom crap into this house. Leave it where you were all afternoon."

"Or what?" He swayed.

"Or someone's going to have to leave," I said.

He moved more quickly than could be expected through the dining room, and with a vice grip left hand, he grabbed me by the throat and pushed me against the wall. "You think you can take me," he shouted. "You don't have a fecking chance."

"Fists aren't the only things that work. I'm telling you to leave my sisters alone."

His physical dominance over his family was his power, and now I knew it.

He stared at me with the angry eyes of an Irishman who had been challenged by someone who had been a disappointment to him his whole life: Not good enough in basketball, not tough enough, didn't have enough women, and had even given up his best sport, baseball. Nothing his oldest son had ever done had impressed him so far.

I guess he didn't know how much I could drink.

I assessed the situation, and, yes, even with a heart condition, even in his sixties, even wobbly drunk, I didn't think I could take him, but I was willing to give it a shot, because Nancy had had my back my whole life.

My mother stepped in, and he let go of me. He looked

at Mum and said, "Make me some eggs."

I walked into the other room, where Nancy remained on the steps.

"Why don't you go ahead home? You don't have to put up with this shit anymore," I said.

While my father sat quietly now eating his eggs in starved embarrassment, I took the car keys from the wall, walked out the back door and started for town.

I drove into Milford and up Purchase Street. Where our home had been, now a vacant area of woods stretched to where a condominium complex called Shadowbrook was being planned. I drove into the field adjacent to the spot that had been our back yard. The shack that had been behind the house still stood, but nothing else. A new house had been erected where ours had been torn down, and the barn was a pile of rubble.

I envisioned my old man telling me how we were supposed to be warriors. I could almost hear him saying, "The Hourihans were the protectors of the kings of Ireland." It brought to me visions of swords and horses and warriors standing their ground.

I remembered the night of the poker game where I got to play and where Davey had told me, "A man stands up."

To the left of where I stood were the woods where my friends and I walked off, armed to the teeth to fight Indians, cowboys, Japs, and Germans, or just play cops and robbers.

I could almost see us walking off into the granite hole armed with guns, knives, axes, and bows and arrows. In front of me was the spot where our barn had been, where my father had religiously taught me to box.

I thought of my second home, St. Mary's, where I had been told I was a soldier of Jesus. I had been happy back then. My mother was right. Back then I believed in something. That was gone.

I had to do something now.

And it occurred to me what I had to do.

Chapter Thirteen
DECISIONS, DECISIONS, DECISIONS

I COULD ONLY DO one thing.

I drove to Worcester on Monday morning. Everything I had thought of in the past week still wedged into my head. I knew what had made me happy before, and I was going to do it again.

I walked into the administration office at Whoopie J and caught the eye of the young girl who seemed to run the place.

"If I drop out, do I get any money back?" I asked.

"Yes," she said. "Well, part of it."

"Okay, make the check out to Patricia Jakola."

Check in hand, I drove to Rutland and left it on the kitchen table, and then I drove back to Milford. I walked into the Town Hall and straight down the stairs to the Air Force recruiter's office. My uncle Frankie had been in the

Air Force and had told me how the Air Force had faster rank, better pay, better accommodations, better food, and in the Air Force you were much less likely to be killed.

The Air Force recruiter was out to lunch, so I joined the Army.

The Army recruiter had me take a two-page test, and when I finished, he corrected it.

"Wait a minute," he said, as he finished double-checking my answers against his answer sheet. His head turned back and forth from the test to the answer sheet, as if he was watching a very small tennis match. When he finished, he went back and corrected it again.

"Well, that's a first for me," he said finally.

I had no idea what he meant. "What?"

"You didn't get anything wrong. You could probably get into the ASA."

"What's that?"

"Well, think, the military arm of NSA."

"What's that?"

"The National Security Agency. It's like spies and stuff like that."

"Right, put me in that."

"Are you sure? I mean, it's a four-year hitch."

"Yeah, so? I figure I'll be in for thirty years and retire with a full pension.'"

"The money part you know, the test part you know, but you never heard of the NSA? Okay. If you wait a few minutes, I'll get the papers." He shook his head and walked off into the back room.

I filled out the papers and signed up for the Army Security Agency to be "a spy and stuff like that."

I drove home and told my mother. She had been vacuuming. I motioned for her to shut it off so I could talk to her, and when I explained that I was going to be a spy for four years in the Army, she kind of shook her head and turned the vacuum cleaner back on. I guess her life hadn't been going exactly how she had planned, either.

My reporting date was to be October eighteenth, one day after my nineteenth birthday.

A week before I had to leave, Pete, Mike, and I were sitting in the Oldsmobile on the one-way street in the center of town, when Mike noticed something near the front door to the Community House. There was a Boy Scout meeting going on inside, and all the bikes were lined up outside the door.

"Those aren't orderly enough for the Army," Mike said.

Before I could stop them, my two friends bolted from the car and were headed for the bikes.

I watched as they piled the bicycles one on top of the other until they'd created a twenty-foot-high pile of bikes, and they were now getting a running start and throwing them up on top.

Since I was shipping out a few days later, the police wished me well and told me it would be "a very bad idea" for me to miss my bus.

Mike and Pete had to repair any bicycles that had been damaged and pay for the ones that couldn't be fixed. One of the bikes had belonged to the younger brother of my new girlfriend. Her father now hated me.

A few days later, in a large sunlit room, in the Boston Army Base, with hundreds of young men in white underwear waiting to do their duty for God and country and become John Wayne type heroes fighting for God and the American way, I stood against the wall waiting to be called. We had just finished our three-minute physicals when another man, this one in an Army uniform, walked into the room.

"Line up maggots!" he screamed, and it echoed off the walls, just in case we hadn't heard it.

I thought, *Who the hell is that?*

"I said line up, you lower-than-the-Army-mule piss ants!"

Holy shit, I thought. *He means me.*

We all jumped to our feet and filled in a line that the screamer started by grabbing one short guy by the arm and pulling him to a space near one wall. "Start here!" he shouted.

The line grew from there, across the room, down along the wall, and up the other side.

"Step out of line if you are volunteers!" the guy shouted. That was me and about a quarter of the young men in line. We were Regular Army, so we got to return to cowering in our places near the far wall.

A Marine sergeant ceremoniously walked in from the adjacent room and began walking down the line, counting the draftees by shouting a number and pointing at their chests.

"One, Two, Three, Marine. One, Two, Three, Marine." Down the line, the bigger boys started counting to see if they were to be a number or a Marine. The shuffling began, the tougher kids shoving the smaller ones into the line to become Marines.

At one point, the sergeant stopped his counting and almost ran down the line to a large boy who had just adjusted the lineup, and he pointed right in the kid's face. "You," he said. "You're a Marine."

"No fucking way," the kid answered.

"Arrest him, and put him on the bus," the counter said, and two Marine SPs did exactly what they had been told.

I couldn't help thinking, *Wow, not what I expected.*

I thought maybe I could just walk out the back door and get on a city bus home, but then I saw that the MPs I had seen at the doors were actually there to keep us in.

"Alright," shouted the first guy, not the Marine, "All you assholes who signed up, put your clothes on and follow me. Draftees stay here."

"Where are we going?" someone asked.

"You're going to Fort Dix Basic Training. Where did you think you were going, asshole?"

Hours later, in the middle of the night, we were herded off the bus at Fort Dix, New Jersey. We were pushed and cajoled into lines. We hadn't eaten since morning. We were lost and disoriented, and this guy, who everyone later called Froggy because of his stature and his voice, kept shouting things at us.

"You will need to know everything I tell you right now. You will be tested on it tomorrow. You are one step below the Army mule. You are E-nothings. You are not humans. You are maggots. You will be maggots until you are told otherwise. Do you understand, maggots?"

"Yes, sir," the group of about fifty shouted.

"Sir? I'm not an officer. My parents were married. I am a Sergeant. You will say, yes Sergeant. Say it, maggots!"

"Yes Sergeant," most of them shouted.

His voice drifted off as I realized he was lying. There would be no test. This was the test, and it didn't matter if we failed. He was just killing time and getting us really tired so no one would have the strength to run away.

A kid in front of me wavered. I saw his knees buckle, and he went down.

"Lay down, Slick," Froggy shouted. "Don't get up, you weak maggot!"

I leaned over toward the prone boy.

"Don't help that maggot! Leave him where he belongs — on the ground with the other maggots!"

More gave out and hit the ground, and each time he said the same thing, "Lay down, Slick!"

It went on into the night until, mercifully, Froggy said something different.

"Left face! Forward march!"

None of us really knew what that meant, but we did turn to the left and walk off into the night.

We were herded through the blackness by a guy with a

flashlight. We followed him like a herd of obedient dogs to a row of barracks, and each group of about twenty was directed to our new "transit" home.

Sleep, the only defense mechanism we had left, came immediately.

The next morning arrived before the sun. We were screamed awake, rushed into the mess hall, fed our breakfast, and rushed back out into the company street to await orders. Today we got our first uniforms, boots, hats, gloves, jackets, and overcoats. We were also handed a cardboard box.

Back at the barracks, we were told what the boxes were for.

As I stuffed all of my civilian clothing and belongings into the box, including the black and white parka my mother had just bought me this year, something strange happened.

My eyes watered. I tried to hide it from the others but realized it wasn't necessary. Most of them were trying to hide it too. Sending your civilian clothes home turned out to be the moment we understood we had become a helpless ward of the federal government. That bastard who shouted at us and called us maggots, he was both my mother and father now. This would take some reassessing.

That night, I decided that this was not what I had signed up for. Someone, even if it had been just the black and white movies of the fifties and sixties, had lied to us.

We had been issued our olive drab, permanent fatigue

uniforms with white name tags and everything. In our anonymity, they had at least given us back our names.

A few days later, in the morning, a guy named Hoyt and I were in line for "chow" as we had been told to call our breakfast, when a guy with a yellow stripe on his arm walked up to us. We were still "in transit," not yet in Basic Training. Having a stripe on your arm meant you were not a trainee like us. Instead, you had finished training, and you were now stationed here. This made you imminently powerful.

"You two," he said.

We turned to him. "What?" I said.

"You get to be on work details. Follow me!" With certainty that his order would be followed by two people who had recently endured a night with Froggy, he turned and began to walk away.

I got Hoyt's attention and pointed to the name tag that had been sewn onto our left breast pockets.

"He doesn't know who we are," I said, covering the name tag. "Let's go."

We placed our hands over our hearts and ran like hell. Hoyt followed me, laughing.

The stripe-guy didn't know what to do, and the best he could muster was, "Hey, come back here."

We didn't have breakfast until later, but we didn't have to go on work details, either.

It occurred to me that instead of the pretense of life in Hopedale, the pretense that everyone was being treated fairly, while in fact some were being singled out for different treatment, the reality at Fort Dix was everyone was obviously being treated like shit. It wasn't personal.

This I could deal with.

I was in Victor Company. We were taught a little ditty that we could shout whenever we were told to. It went, "Victor, V-I-C-T-O-R, Second to none, We'll get it done. We'll sweat in blood. Kill!" I didn't say it much.

One morning, standing in line for chow, a fight broke out. Mario was a tough kid from Providence, Rhode Island. For some reason, or no reason at all, he grabbed a skinny kid in front of him by the shirt and shoved him against the side of the mess hall. The kid was probably the least likely person on Fort Dix to become an actual soldier. Before the fight began, its outcome had been determined, or it would have been if I hadn't found myself stepping into the middle.

I pushed Hannigan away and turned toward the bigger boy.

"What?" Mario asked. "You think you can take me, Hourihan?"

"No. I doubt that a whole lot, but I can't let you just beat the crap out of him. I think I can probably take more than he can."

"I like you Hourihan, so I'm going tell you, don't ever do that again. You're off the hook, Hannigan. Thank your buddy here."

In line inside the building, more than a few trainees thanked me, and while I ate, Sergeant Malone, our platoon sergeant, walked by our table and slapped me on the back.

In about the fifth week of our eight-week Basic

Training was the first time I had ever fired a rifle, so it was a surprise to most everyone when I had the best scores in the company, and my platoon got a weekend pass, which we used to go to the Post Exchange to drink 3.2 beer.

It wasn't my expertise with an M-14 that got us the pass, however. It was the brilliance of a friend named Frank James. Frank was six-foot-five, about two hundred pounds and a proud young black man from the unfriendly streets of Newark, New Jersey. The thing with Mario made Frank decide he liked me. He started looking after me, and when it came to the rifle range, he had an idea.

"Hour hand," he said. "Let's get us a couple days off."

"Who do I have to kill?"

"No one. Matter of fact, you don't have to do anything other than you would do anyways. When we get to our test at the rifle range, you make sure you are in line right next to me."

"Why?"

"Because, whoever gets the high individual score gets a weekend off for his whole platoon."

"I'm not that good a shot," I said.

"No, *you're* not, but *we* are," James answered.

We both shot at the same targets, mine. I got a tremendous score. James not so much, but there wasn't any punishment for having a low score. We figured it might have even kept him out of the infantry.

Then, after the eight weeks were up, the night before we would all head home on leave, Victor Company trainees sat cross-legged on the perfectly waxed and buffed floor of the day room somewhere in the middle of Fort Dix. Sgt. Malone, the giant black man, and Sgt. Callahan, a short, fireplug, blond crew cut Irishman, stood in front of us.

Malone, our head drill sergeant, spoke.

"Now that yous have put in your eight weeks' time, yous mens is on a even par with the Army mule," he said. I had spoken with Malone before. This was not how he talked. He was faking stupidity. He had told me weeks before that discipline, making sure the troops would obey what the ranking man told them to do, that they would obey the rank regardless of the man wearing it, was the only way to cut through the fog of war.

In this meeting we would each find out where we would be transferred for advanced training, but first he read off a list of names who had received accelerated promotions.

I stood up with the rest of the ten percent of the company who, for one reason or another, had just become E2 privates, a step above the damn mule. Everyone would catch up as soon as they got to their next duty station, but we "elite" would get an extra month's raise in pay. This was good, since my first paycheck had been sixty-eight dollars.

My test grades had put me in the Army Security Agency, a military arm of NSA. When Malone got to reading my orders, he lapsed out of his practiced air of feigned stupidity into just being himself.

"Well, Private Hourihan, we have some good news, some better news, and some not so good news." He smiled at me. It was his recommendation that had afforded me the promotion. I assumed it was for being the top marksman in our company. "Your tests put you in the top three percent of the Army.... Further testing put you in the Defense Language Institute in California." He lowered the papers he read from. "That's the top one percent of the Army, trainee... I'm impressed, and here is the not so good part. You'll be studying Vietnamese."

His eyebrows raised.

I had no idea what made this such a bad thing and asked, "What the hell is Viennese? I didn't ask for that. I asked for French."

A murmur turned quickly into laughter by all those other recruits who were not in the top one percent or even the top three percent. All those "dummies" knew where Vietnam was, unlike those of us who had been educated in an inadequate, pompous for no apparent reason education system taught by teachers, many of whom hid the world from us while they plied their own prejudices and biases and got us ready for work in the foundry of The Diamond D, Draper Corporation. At least that's what I blamed it on, rather than my own stupidity. Malone called it, "ASA, Assholes who'll Sign Anything."

It dawned on me in a particularly frigid mid-December evening, in the day room of Victor Company, Fort Dix, that I had just signed up for four years in the U.S. Army in 1965, and I didn't even know that we were at war. Guess I wasn't paying attention. But now, at least, I understood what those kids from Clark University were shouting about. I wanted a do over, but it was too late.

Our second drill instructor, Sgt Callahan, stepped up

and incredulously shouted, "You be in this man's army, headed for Vietnam, and you don't know where it is? Tell me boy that you know we are at war! Tell me you isn't that fucking stupid! Please, tell me you knew!"

I hadn't.

"I do now, Sarge."

Every trainee laughed. Both DIs laughed. I laughed. It wasn't funny.

And my first rule in the Army was born. Have a sense of humor and play the cards you're dealt.

I drank away a month of leave in the town where I had dodged or been hidden from the knowledge that my country was at war in Vietnam, and I headed for Monterey, California to learn the language of our enemy, because I was so smart.

The day I left, my sister Pat cornered me in the kitchen in the morning.

"We need to talk," she said.

I sat down and waited.

"There is a war going on in Vietnam." She hesitated. "People are being killed. You know that, don't you?"

I thought for a few seconds and then answered. "Of course I do. Do you think I'm stupid?"

After six weeks or so of trying my best to flunk out of the Defense Language Institute West Coast, myself and a handful of others with similar ideas were called in. The Major explained, "We can't flunk you out. It would be better for you if you learned the language. Get out of my office!"

I set up chairs for the Monterey Music Festival — made

ten bucks, got recruited by a Baha'i girl with a great body until she realized I was only in the religion for her. I met a Playboy bunny on the beach who tried to teach me to surf and then took me to a beach party where the guitar-playing singer among the fifteen or so partiers was Joan Baez. I traveled California on the back of a Yamaha motorcycle, Yosemite to Salinas to Big Sur. Saw Elizabeth Taylor at a restaurant on Cannery Row. I got promoted again, spent whole days sunning on Carmel Beach, and tried to drink the Enlisted Men's Club dry. Then my Top Secret, Crypto, codeword, security clearance came in. I was going to be an electronic spy and stuff.

On leave at home, on a particularly warm and decidedly marijuana-mind-altered afternoon with Mike and Peter, my best friends in Hopedale, we pulled the car into a restaurant parking lot, slid down the steep grass-and-dirt hill to the water and went swimming in a lake beside the highway. While Mike and Peter swam, my attention was taken by two girls on the bank. I made my way to shore, sat on a shore rock and talked with them for a few minutes. I found out that the blond was named "Spooky" and the pretty dark-haired one with the teal blue eyes lived in the red house on the hill across the highway, when my friends came and grabbed me and told me it was time to go. "She's like twelve years old," Pete warned. That I hadn't noticed, so we left, and I went back to California.

In the meantime in Monterey, I learned the damn language and said my goodbyes. It was tough to leave the girl I was dating, and my family, but the rest was easy.

In San Angelo, Texas, where I spent two months being taught about "security," I got a job singing at the Gas Light Lounge of a Ramada Inn. They paid me in beer until it got too costly, and they decided to pay me fifty dollars a performance to save money. After the two months, I packed my duffel bag and got ready to go to their war — Private First Class Hourihan. Vietnamese linguist, just playing the cards I was dealt.

And, after a thirty-day leave, I got comfortable in the back seat of our family car, on the way to Logan Airport, I took in the gray overcast sky, and realized, just as the nuns had told me would happen, I was literally being put in a box and sent to China — well, French Indo-China.

In Boston, I stepped out onto the sidewalk in front of the terminal, and I said goodbye to my family again.

My father called me aside before I entered the terminal.

"Did you hear about the dog who tried to run across the tracks in front of a train?" he asked.

"What?"

"The train cut off his tail."

"Okay," I said, not knowing what he was talking about.

"Then he went back to get his tail and another train came and cut off his head." He smiled at me. "You know the moral of the story?"

"No," I said.

He smiled and moved to where he could look directly into my eyes. "The moral is, don't lose your head over a piece of tail."

I smiled and nodded. Picked up my bag and headed for

the terminal.

I was numb and alone as I stood in line to check in, rolling my duffle bag ahead with one foot. As I reached the next-in-line spot, I could see myself in the shining chrome of the airline kiosk. I was dressed in a dark green uniform with a yellow stripe on either arm, my hat was tucked under my arm, my black low-quarter shoes spit shined, and my head was shaved bald. I had put on thirty pounds of muscle in Basic Training, and I didn't look anything like me.

It occurred to me more seriously than it had ever before, that I was a soldier headed to war.

It might be the last place I existed.

I may truly never see my parents or family again, just like Sister Mary Patrick had said.

I asked myself quietly, almost as a whimper, "What the hell have I done?"

I stepped onto the plane and headed for Saigon — wherever the hell that was.

Coming Soon...

Baltimore Catechism: Sacrament of Reconciliation

Book Four in the Baltimore Catechism series

About the Author

John T. Hourihan Jr., a retired journalist, has won state, regional and national awards for his opinion column in several New England newspapers. He received the Cross of Gallantry for valor in Vietnam, where he served three tours as a Vietnamese linguist. He is disabled now from the effects of Agent Orange. He lives with his author wife Lin Hourihan (*The Virtue of Virtues*, *The Mystery of the Sturbridge Keys*) in the woods of central Massachusetts. His other works include *Baltimore Catechism: Clean Slate*, *Baltimore Catechism: Year of Confirmation*, *The Mustard Seed – 2095*, *The Mustard Seed – 2110*, *The Mustard Seed – 2130*, *Beyond the Fence*: *Converging Memoirs*, *Parables for a New Age I and II*, *Play Fair and Win*.